LEWIS CARROLL

Modern Critical Views

These and other titles in preparation

Modern Critical Views

LEWIS CARROLL

Edited and with an introduction by
Harold Bloom
Sterling Professor of the Humanities
Yale University

CHELSEA HOUSE PUBLISHERS
New York ◊ New Haven ◊ Philadelphia

© 1987 by Chelsea House Publishers, a division of Chelsea House
Educational Communications, Inc.

3 5 7 9 8 6 4 2

Introduction © 1987 by Harold Bloom

Printed and bound in the United States of America

∞ The paper used in this publication meets the minimum re-
quirements of the American National Standard for Permanence of
Paper for Printed Library Materials, Z39.48–1984.

Library of Congress Cataloging-in-Publication Data

Lewis Carroll.

  (Modern critical views)
  Bibliography: p.
  Includes index.
  Contents: Ironic voyage / Robert Martin Adams—The Alice
books and the metaphors of Victorian childhood / Jan B. Gordon—
Alice and Wonderland / Nina Auerbach—[etc.]
  1. Carroll, Lewis, 1832–1898—Criticism and
interpretation.   2. Children's stories, English—History and
criticism. [1. Carroll, Lewis, 1832–1898—Criticism and interpretation.   2. English literature—History and
criticism]   I. Bloom, Harold.   II. Series.
PR4612.L452   1987   828'.809   86–20736
ISBN 0–87754–689–4 (alk. paper)

Contents

Editor's Note

This book brings together a representative selection of the best literary criticism devoted to the writings of Lewis Carroll, arranged in the chronological order of its original publication. I am grateful to Susan Laity for her erudition and judgment in helping to edit this volume.

My introduction centers upon the peculiar nature of Carroll's enigmatic or riddling allegory, with its acting principle that, in Wonderland, time has been murdered. Robert Martin Adams begins the chronological sequence with a brief but pungent description of the quest of *The Hunting of the Snark* as a search for Nothing. In a study of metaphor in the *Alice* books, Jan B. Gordon reads a series of self-conscious responses to an absence of self as the pattern that underlies Carroll's figurative vision of childhood.

Nina Auerbach, working from a perspective of feminist literary criticism, explores "the anomaly of Carroll's Alice, who explodes out of Wonderland hungry and unregenerate." This primordial Alice, a field in which the drives have their interplay, is very different from "the philosopher's *Alice*" of Peter Heath, who finds Carroll's professional passion for the study of logic to be very much at the center of the *Alice* books.

The *Sylvie and Bruno* books are analyzed by Edmund Miller as a return to the earlier Victorian novel of Charlotte Brontë's sort, in which the author's faith in coincidence reflects a conviction that "God orders our lives with love." Again, a very different viewpoint—semiotic and psychoanalytical—is represented by Alwin L. Baum, who finds that *Alice*'s passages "lead into the edenic garden of paradox, the key to which is language itself."

Judith Crews intricately traces the "plain superficiality" of Carroll's "game of names," while Edward Guiliano more plainly states the profound laughter and despair of that intricate enigma, *The Hunting of the Snark*. In an overview of the erotic universe of the *Alice* books, Donald Rackin explores Carroll's implicit dialectic of love and death, or the dualism uncovered by Freud in his final theory of the drives. *Through the Looking-Glass*, that marvelous anatomy of mixed verse and prose, is seen by Beverly Lyon Clark as an interaction of poem and narrative that "hints at a more serious questioning of reality."

This book concludes with an extraordinary essay on Carroll's version of quest romance by the poet John Hollander, which is published here for the first time. Illuminating the rather obscure notion of "nonsense verse," Hollander concentrates upon the dominant force of the quest itself, a force that returns Carroll to the true power of Spenserian romance, and to the equivocal pathos of all human romance.

Introduction

I

*"And yet what a dear little puppy it was!" said Alice, as she leant against
a buttercup to rest herself, and fanned herself with one of the leaves. "I
should have liked teaching it tricks very much, if—if I'd only been the right
size to do it! Oh dear! I'd nearly forgotten that I've got to grow up again!"*

Whatever the process is of renewing one's experience of *Alice's Adventures in
Wonderland, Through the Looking-Glass,* and *The Hunting of the Snark,* the
sensation is neither that of rereading nor of reading as though for the first time.
Lewis Carroll is Shakespearean to the degree that his writing has become a kind
of Scripture for us. Take, quite at random, the sublimely outrageous chapter 6,
"Pig and Pepper," of *Alice's Adventures in Wonderland.* Alice enters a large,
smoky kitchen and discovers an atmosphere permeated with pepper, a sneezing
Duchess, and a howling and sneezing baby, as well as a cook stirring a cauldron
of soup, and a large, grinning Cheshire Cat. Carroll's prevalent phantasmagoria
heightens (if that is possible) as the cook commences to throw everything
within her reach (fire-irons, saucepans, dishes) at the Duchess and her howling
imp, while the Duchess cries out: "Chop off her head!" and sings a sort of
lullaby to her baby, thoughtfully shaking it (violently) at the end of each line:

> "Speak roughly to your little boy,
>   And beat him when he sneezes:
> He only does it to annoy,
>   Because he knows it teases."
>
> CHORUS
> (in which the cook and the baby joined): —
>   "Wow! wow! wow!"

While the Duchess sang the second verse of the song, she kept tossing the baby violently up and down, and the poor little thing howled so, that Alice could hardly hear the words: —

> "I speak severely to my boy,
>   And beat him when he sneezes:
> For he can thoroughly enjoy
>   The pepper when he pleases!"

CHORUS
"Wow! wow! wow!"

"Here! You may nurse it a bit, if you like!" the Duchess said to Alice, flinging the baby at her as she spoke. "I must go and get ready to play croquet with the Queen," and she hurried out of the room. The cook threw a frying-pan after her as she went, but it just missed her.

Carroll stated the parodist's principle as choosing the best poems for model, but here the paradigm is a ghastly children's poem of the mid-nineteenth century:

> Speak gently to the little child!
>   Its love be sure to gain;
> Teach it in accents soft and mild;
>   It may not long remain.

That is ghastly enough to be its own parody, but Carroll wants it for his own dark purposes. The pepper is peculiarly analogous to a sexual stimulant, and the boy baby turns out to be a pig (presumably because little boys were not the objects of Carroll's affections). Alice, like Carroll, has no use for them:

So she set the little creature down, and felt quite relieved to see it trot away quietly into the wood. "If it had grown up," she said to herself, "it would have made a dreadfully ugly child: but it makes rather a handsome pig, I think." And she began thinking over other children she knew, who might do very well as pigs, and was just saying to herself, "if one only knew the right way to change them—" when she was a little startled by seeing the Cheshire Cat sitting on a bough of a tree a few yards off.

The Cheshire Cat is an ironic enigma, typical of many such in Carroll's enigmatic or riddling allegory. He is thoroughly unpleasant, but so, generally, are many of the inhabitants of Wonderland. It is a truism of criticism to remark that the child Alice is considerably more mature than any of the inhabitants of Wonderland, but what the Cheshire Cat remarks is true also:

> The Cat only grinned when it saw Alice. It looked good-natured, she thought: still it had *very* long claws and a great many teeth, so she felt that it ought to be treated with respect.
>
> "Cheshire Puss," she began, rather timidly, as she did not at all know whether it would like the name: however, it only grinned a little wider. "Come, it's pleased so far," thought Alice, and she went on. "Would you tell me, please, which way I ought to go from here?"
>
> "That depends a good deal on where you want to get to," said the Cat.
>
> "I don't much care where—" said Alice.
>
> "Then it doesn't matter which way you go," said the Cat.
>
> "—so long as I get *somewhere*," Alice added as an explanation.
>
> "Oh, you're sure to do that," said the Cat, "if you only walk long enough."
>
> Alice felt that this could not be denied, so she tried another question. "What sort of people live about here?"
>
> "In *that* direction," the Cat said, waving its right paw round, "lives a Hatter: and in *that* direction," waving the other paw, "lives a March Hare. Visit either you like: they're both mad."
>
> "But I don't want to go among mad people," Alice remarked.
>
> "Oh, you can't help that," said the Cat: "we're all mad here. I'm mad. You're mad."
>
> "How do you know I'm mad?" said Alice.
>
> "You must be," said the Cat, "or you wouldn't have come here."
>
> Alice didn't think that proved it at all: however, she went on: "And how do you know that you're mad?"
>
> "To begin with," said the Cat, "a dog's not mad. You grant that?"
>
> "I suppose so," said Alice.
>
> "Well, then," the Cat went on, "you see a dog growls when it's angry, and wags its tail when it's pleased. Now *I* growl when I'm pleased, and wag my tail when I'm angry. Therefore I'm mad."
>
> "*I* call it purring, not growling," said Alice.

Is Alice mad, because she has come to Wonderland? When the Cheshire

Cat reappears, it stages a famously slow vanishing, ending with its grin, which stays on for some time after the rest of it is gone. That ontological grin is the emblem of the Cheshire Cat's madness, and is the prelude to the Mad Tea Party of the next chapter, which in turn is emblematical of the *Alice* books, since they can be described, quite accurately, as a mad tea party, rather than a nonsensical tea party. Lionel Trilling spoke of "the world of nonsense, that curious invention of the English of the nineteenth century, of Lewis Carroll and Edward Lear," and confessed that, critically, nonsense seemed to him inexplicable: "One of the mysteries of art, perhaps as impenetrable as why tragedy gives pleasure, is why nonsense commands so fascinated an attention, and why, when it succeeds, it makes more than sense."

A critic as distinguished as Trilling, William Empson, sought to solve the mystery by finding a defense against madness in Alice's characteristic stance:

> Much of the technique of the rudeness of the Mad Hatter has been learned from Hamlet. It is the ground-bass of this kinship with insanity, I think, that makes it so clear that the books are not trifling, and the cool courage with which Alice accepts madmen that gives them their strength.
>
> ("The Child as Swain," *Some Versions of Pastoral*)

It does not seem to me either that Carroll makes nonsense into "more than sense" or that Alice's undoubted courage is particularly cool. Unlike the sublime Edward Lear, Carroll does not read to me as a nonsense writer. Riddle is not nonsense, and enigmatic allegory does not exalt courage as the major virtue. Carroll is a Victorian Romantic just as were his exact contemporaries, the Pre-Raphaelite poets, but his phantasmagoria, utterly unlike theirs, is a wholly successful defense against, or revision of, High Romantic Quest. Christina Rossetti's *Goblin Market* has more in common with Edward Lear than Carroll does, and Swinburne is an even defter parodist than Carroll.

Carroll's parodies, sometimes brilliant though they are, do not transcend their echoes, do not reverse Carroll's own burden of literary belatedness. But the *Alice* books and *The Hunting of the Snark* do achieve convincing originality, while the Pre-Raphaelites sometimes are merely involuntary parodies of Keats, Shelley, Tennyson, and Browning. Romantic erotic quest, which ends in the Inferno of Shelley's *The Triumph of Life*, is displaced into the purgatorial sadomasochism of the Pre-Raphaelite poets. Dante Gabriel Rossetti, Swinburne, and their critical follower, Pater, substitute or trope the body for time, and accept the violence of the will's revenge against time upon their own bodies.

Carroll evades both sadomasochism and the Romantic erotic quest by identifying himself with the seven-year-old Alice. Wonderland has only one reality principle, which is that time has been murdered. Nothing need be substituted for time, even though only madness can murder time. Alice is only as mad as she needs to be, which may be her actual legacy from Hamlet. She will not grow up, or sexually mature, so long as she can get back into Wonderland, and she can get back out of Wonderland whenever she needs to. The Pre-Raphaelites and Pater are immersed in the world of the reality principle, the world of Schopenhauer and Freud. Psychoanalytic interpretations of Carroll's works always fail, because they are necessarily easy and vulgar, and therefore disgusting. Alice does not deign to be told what she is evading, and Carroll's books are not exercises in sublimation. What is repressed in them is his discomfort with culture, including Wordsworth, the largest precursor of his vision.

II

"Hold your tongue!" said the Queen, turning purple.

"I won't!" said Alice.

"Off with her head!" the Queen shouted at the top of her voice. Nobody moved.

"Who cares for *you*?" said Alice (she had grown to her full size by this time). "You're nothing but a pack of cards!"

This is the crisis of *Alice's Adventures in Wonderland*; it asserts Alice's freedom from her own phantasmagoria, after which she returns to our order of reality. The parallel moment in *Through the Looking-Glass* is a weak repetition of this splendor:

There was not a moment to be lost. Already several of the guests were lying down in the dishes, and the soup-ladle was walking up the table towards Alice's chair, and beckoning to her impatiently to get out of its way.

"I can't stand this any longer!" she cried, as she jumped up and seized the tablecloth with both hands: one good pull, and plates, dishes, guests, and candles came crashing down together in a heap on the floor.

The movement from "You're nothing but a pack of cards!" to "I can't stand this any longer!" is a fair representation of the relative aesthetic decline the reader experiences as she goes from *Alice's Adventures in Wonderland* to *Through the Looking-Glass*. Had the first book never existed, our regard for the second would be unique and immense, which is only another way of admiring how the first *Alice* narrative is able to avoid any human affect as mundane as bitterness. The White Rabbit is an extraordinary parody of Carroll's own sense of literary and even erotic belatedness, yet the quality he conveys is an exuberant vivacity. We are, all of us, now perpetually late for a very important date, but that apprehension of being late, late is for many among us an anxious expectation. For Carroll, in his first vision as Alice, everything is again early, which gives the book its pure and radiant atmosphere of a triumphant firstness.

Bitterness keeps breaking in as we read *Through the Looking-Glass*, which may explain how weirdly and perpetually contemporary this second and somewhat lesser work now seems. Its epitome is that grand poem, "The Walrus and the Carpenter":

> " 'But wait a bit,' the Oysters cried,
>   'Before we have our chat;
> For some of us are out of breath,
>   And all of us are fat!'
> 'No hurry!' said the Carpenter.
>   They thanked him much for that.
>
> 'A loaf of bread,' the Walrus said,
>   'Is what we chiefly need:
> Pepper and vinegar besides
>   Are very good indeed—
> Now, if you're ready, Oysters dear,
>   We can begin to feed.'
>
> 'But not on us!' the Oysters cried,
>   Turning a little blue.
> 'After such kindness, that would be
>   A dismal thing to do!'
> 'The night is fine,' the Walrus said.
>   'Do you admire the view?
>
> 'It was so kind of you to come!
>   And you are very nice!'
> The Carpenter said nothing but
>   'Cut us another slice.
> I wish you were not quite so deaf—
>   I've had to ask you twice!'
>
> 'It seems a shame,' the Walrus said,
>   'To play them such a trick.

After we've brought them out so far,
   And made them trot so quick!'
The Carpenter said nothing but
   'The butter's spread too thick!'

'I weep for you,' the Walrus said:
   'I deeply sympathize.'
With sobs and tears he sorted out
   Those of the largest size,
Holding his pocket-handkerchief
   Before his streaming eyes.

'O Oysters,' said the Carpenter,
   'You've had a pleasant run!
Shall we be trotting home again?'
   But answer came there none—
And this was scarcely odd, because
   They'd eaten every one."

In an additional stanza, written for a theatrical presentation of the *Alice* narratives, but fortunately not part of our received text, Carroll accuses the Walrus and the Carpenter of "craft and cruelty," a judgment in which Alice joins him when she remarks that "They were *both* very unpleasant characters—." But so are the Sheep, and that pompous egg-head Humpty Dumpty, though we do not receive them as quite the weird representations that actually they indeed constitute. Carroll's art renders each of them as totally idiosyncratic, it being Carroll's largest enigma that only Alice, in either book, lacks personality or pathos. In "The Walrus and the Carpenter," those two voracious deceivers are neatly distinguished from one another. They are both weepers, high Victorian sentimentalists, living in a contra-natural midnight world where the sun outshines the sulky moon, presumably an indication that this world oddly is natural —all-too-natural—which is to say: hungry.

The Walrus and the Carpenter weep to increase their appetites, as it were, but the Walrus, being the orator of the two, is finally so moved by his own eloquence that he weeps on, even when he is happily satiated. Though he is more cunning than the Carpenter, he is also less sadistic; we wince a bit at the Carpenter's "Shall we be trotting home again?" but we ought to wince more when the Walrus sobbingly says: "I weep for you. I deeply sympathize."

Humpty Dumpty may well be Carroll's most famous enigma, and his most Shakespearean. He is also a prophecy of many of our contemporary literary theorists: "I can explain all the poems that ever were invented — and a good many that haven't been invented just yet." "You're so exactly like other people," Humpty Dumpty rather nastily says to Alice, but he receives his comeuppance just as she pronounces her accurate normative judgment that he is truly "unsatisfactory."

The White Knight, at once the most satisfactory and charmingly pleasant of Carroll's enigmas, is the figure in *Through the Looking-Glass* who returns us vividly to the gentler spirit of *Alice's Adventures in Wonderland*. There is a critical tradition that the White Knight is a self-portrait of Charles Lutwidge Dodgson, the other self of Lewis Carroll in the world of the reality principle. There may be something to this, but more palpably the White Knight is a version of the kindly, heroic, and benignly mad Don Quixote. The White Knight's madness is like Alice's own malady, if the Cheshire Cat was right about Alice. It is the madness of play, Carroll's sweet madness, a defense against darker madness.

Carroll's best poem ever is "The White Knight's Ballad," which is a superb and loving parody of Wordsworth's great crisis-poem "Resolution and Independence." Wordsworth's near-solipsism, his inability to listen to what the old Leech-gatherer is saying in answer to the poet's anguished question ("How is it that you live, and what is it you do?") was mocked rather mercilessly in Carroll's original version of his poem, published in 1856, fifteen years before *Through the Looking-Glass*. In the 1856 poem, "Upon the Lonely Moor," the poet is outrageously rough and even brutal to the aged man, who is not just unheard but is kicked, punched, boxed on the ear, and has his hair tweaked. All this happily is softened in the beautiful revision that is the song sung by the White Knight:

> "It's long," said the Knight, "but it's very, *very* beautiful. Everybody that hears me sing it — either it brings the *tears* into their eyes, or else —"
>
> "Or else what?" said Alice, for the Knight had made a sudden pause.
>
> "Or else it doesn't, you know. The name of the song is called '*Haddocks' Eyes*.'"
>
> "Oh, that's the name of the song, is it?" Alice said, trying to feel interested.
>
> "No, you don't understand," the Knight said, looking a little vexed. "That's what the name is *called*. The name really *is* '*The Aged Aged Man*.'"
>
> "Then I ought to have said 'That's what the *song* is called'?" Alice corrected herself.
>
> "No, you oughtn't: that's quite another thing! The *song* is called '*Ways And Means*': but that's only what it's *called*, you know!"

"Well, what *is* the song, then?" said Alice, who was by this time completely bewildered.

"I was coming to that," the Knight said. "The song really *is* '*A-sitting On A Gate*': and the tune's my own invention."

So saying, he stopped his horse and let the reins fall on its neck: then, slowly beating time with one hand, and with a faint smile lighting up his gentle foolish face, as if he enjoyed the music of his song, he began.

Of all the strange things that Alice saw in her journey Through The Looking-Glass, this was the one that she always remembered most clearly. Years afterwards she could bring the whole scene back again, as if it had been only yesterday—the mild blue eyes and kindly smile of the Knight—the setting sun gleaming through his hair, and shining on his armour in a blaze of light that quite dazzled her—the horse quietly moving about, with the reins hanging loose on his neck, cropping the grass at her feet—and the black shadows of the forest behind—all this she took in like a picture, as, with one hand shading her eyes, she leant against a tree, watching the strange pair, and listening, in a half-dream, to the melancholy music of the song.

"But the tune *isn't* his own invention," she said to herself: "it's '*I give thee all, I can no more.*'" She stood and listened very attentively, but no tears came into her eyes.

> "I'll tell thee everything I can:
>   There's little to relate.
> I saw an aged aged man,
>   A-sitting on a gate.
> 'Who are you, aged man?' I said.
>   'And how is it you live?'
> And his answer trickled through my head,
>   Like water through a sieve.
>
> He said 'I look for butterflies
>   That sleep among the wheat:
> I make them into mutton-pies,
>   And sell them in the street.
> I sell them unto men,' he said,
>   'Who sail on stormy seas;
> And that's the way I get my bread—
>   A trifle, if you please.'

But I was thinking of a plan
    To dye one's whiskers green,
And always use so large a fan
    That they could not be seen.
So, having no reply to give
    To what the old man said,
I cried 'Come, tell me how you live!'
    And thumped him on the head.

His accents mild took up the tale:
    He said 'I go my ways,
And when I find a mountain-rill,
    I set it in a blaze;
And thence they make a stuff they call
    Rowland's Macassar-Oil—
Yet twopence-halfpenny is all
    They give me for my toil.'

But I was thinking of a way
    To feed oneself on batter,
And so go on from day to day
    Getting a little fatter.
I shook him well from side to side,
    Until his face was blue:
'Come, tell me how you live,' I cried,
    'And what it is you do!'

He said 'I hunt for haddocks' eyes
    Among the heather bright,
And work them into waistcoat-
        buttons
    In the silent night.
And these I do not sell for gold
    Or coin of silvery shine,
But for a copper halfpenny,
    And that will purchase nine."

Thumped and shaken blue, but otherwise undamaged, the aged hunter for haddocks' eyes is a belated but less fearful representative of the reality principle than Wordsworth's Leech-gatherer. As much as the Leech-gatherer, the White Knight's decrepit survivor is "like a man from some far region sent, / To give me human strength, by apt admonishment." The alternative for Carroll, as for Wordsworth, would be despondency and madness, the waning of the poet's youthful joy into a death-in-life. But Carroll, fiercely defending against his own Wordsworthianism, triumphantly makes it new in a final vision of the aged man that is anything but Wordsworthian, because it is pure Wonderland:

> "And now, if e'er by chance I put
>   My fingers into glue,
> Or madly squeeze a right-hand foot
>   Into a left-hand shoe,
> Or if I drop upon my toe
>   A very heavy weight,
> I weep, for it reminds me so
> Of that old man I used to know—
> Whose look was mild, whose speech
>   was slow,
> Whose hair was whiter than the snow,
> Whose face was very like a crow,
> With eyes, like cinders, all aglow,
> Who seemed distracted with his woe,
> Who rocked his body to and fro,
> And muttered mumblingly and low,
> As if his mouth were full of dough,
> Who snorted like a buffalo—
> That summer evening long ago,
>   A-sitting on a gate."

ROBERT MARTIN ADAMS

Ironic Voyage

*T*he Hunting of the Snark (1876), which has become of recent years a much more serious piece of humor than it ever was for the Victorians, imposes on the design of the voyage a new and sinister pattern; it presents Nothing, not as an obstacle to be eluded or a test to be passed, but as a predatory potential of the goal itself. Though the Bellman and his crew have five infallible signs for recognizing Snarks, there is no way to tell a Snark from a Boojum until it is too late—in fact, there is no way at all. This is characteristic of the whole undertaking, in which no means is ever proportioned sensibly to an end. The crew's manifold skills are entirely irrelevant to the task at hand, the ship sails now backwards, now forwards, the Bellman gives contradictory orders and for navigation uses a map which, though pleasantly intelligible, is a perfect and absolute blank:

> "What's the good of Mercator's North Poles and Equators,
> Tropics, Zones, and Meridian Lines?"
> So the Bellman would cry: and the crew would reply,
> "They are merely conventional signs!"

Yet despite this indifference to prudential logic and the elements of natural fact —or more properly because of the comic convention that lucky innocents lead a charmed life—the quest has so far succeeded miraculously. It is of course all quests in one, a tempting of destiny by a crew of sacred imbeciles whose irrational agreement upon a final goal which is all things to all men is no stranger

---

From *Nil: Episodes in the Literary Conquest of Void during the Nineteenth Century.*
© 1966 by Robert Martin Adams. Oxford University Press, 1966.

than their diverse senses of the way to reach it. But if this crew, united merely by the "B's" of their names (a signal instance, this, of what Pope and Professor Lovejoy called the Great Chain of Being), and so identified as essentially a crew of plosives, has prospered so far, it is only that they may be led more rapidly to the culminating disaster, itself a "B." (It is in effect the *but* = end or purpose of which Baudelaire wrote in "Le Voyage," which, "n'étant nulle part, peut être n'importe où.") Emerging from nowhere in response to no summons (like those other fabled voyagers toward a fateful objective, Childe Roland and Captain Ahab), engaged in an insane enterprise looking toward what may be either a vague good or a permanent annihilation, they encounter the last number of their own sequence, the Boojum. Supreme reward (Snark) and ultimate catastrophe (Boojum) are only verbally distinguishable, as eternity is conveniently approached through its likeness to annihilation. And it is the Baker, that sacred idiot who cannot remember his own name, who was warned by his aging uncle against Boojums but could not remember to repeat the warning in English, it is the Baker who is predestined to encounter the Boojum. Void adventuring boldly into the world encounters void, ineluctably—or at least what the Baker encounters, though for others it might be Snark, proves for him Boojum. The eminent Snarxist Martin Gardner defines Boojum in these terms:

> The Boojum is more than death. It is the end of all searching. It is final, absolute extinction. In a literal sense, Carroll's Boojum means nothing at all. It is the void, the great blank emptiness out of which we miraculously emerged; by which we will ultimately be devoured; through which the absurd galaxies spiral and drift endlessly on their nonsense voyages from nowhere to nowhere.
>
> (*The Annotated Snark*, New York, 1962)

That the Baker represents the human race emerging miraculously from the cosmic void will perhaps be felt as a romantic extrapolation from the text; but the presence of void within, behind, and about the poem is of its essence, and there is not really much difference between a medium-sized void and a great big one. The Bellman's venture has neither a starting point nor a coherent method nor an objective; like a pair of violins unaccompanied, its two counterpointed themes, of inconsequence and inevitability, poise with the necessary perilous fragility only when raised over an emptiness. As Milton's Satan makes his way through chaos, so the Bellman and his crew are continually confronted with irrelevance and menaced with a fall; as they mimic the adventures of human life (itself a voyage from void to void), their lunacies are invaded by an abrupt and violent principle of accident which at the end of the poem has taken full command. The Banker can be rescued from the Bandersnatch at the very moderate expense of his sanity, but the Baker's vanishing is ultimate, like that of Oedipus. It implies not merely that the quest is foolish and the man fated, but more exquisitely (like Kafka's fable of the man before the law), that only he could discover the Snark for whom it was bound to prove a Boojum. The conditions of the problem were such as to lead inevitably to the destruction of its solver, while those who were immune to the consequences could not solve it in the first place. The poem's metaphorical action represents two interlocking binds; for obvious reasons, its pattern of self-defeating success has a special fascination for us these days.

Being fantastic, the action of the *Snark* takes place by tacit definition within the realm of an undefined psyche, where one neither expects a consequence nor resists an association. The freedom of assertion first acquired under the protection of "nonsense" writing is now a common liberty of fiction; in effect it permits an elastic, adaptable fable which under new circumstances freely takes on new features. The adventure of the Bellman makes use of physical questing largely for narrative backbone; but as it winds through many appended and incidental voids, void opens before it as a vortex, drawing irresistibly forward and finally swallowing the story's agents. Its ability to release the suggestive power of void is only one of this pleasant poem's pioneering distinctions.

JAN B. GORDON

The Alice *Books and the Metaphors*
of Victorian Childhood

If one had to choose the image most closely associated with the Victorian novel, the orphan would rank high on any list. Although statistics are by no means conclusive, there would appear to have been no greater percentage of orphans among the middle classes that provided the bulk of the audience for the nineteenth-century novel than at any other time in British history. Although child abuses were rampant during the Victorian period, phenomena corresponding to workhouses and chimney sweepers, and surely as malevolent, could be found during almost any period of history. Obviously the child without parental guidance or support exists partially on a metaphoric level. Surely, to probe the popularity of the emblem is to find out how the concept of the child invaded the consciousness of the Victorian era. Although space does not allow a complete exposition of this occurrence, the orphan clearly came to symbolize all the discontinuities that faced the age. As Walter Houghton has astutely observed in *The Victorian Frame of Mind*, the problem of locating a point of origin was one of the continuing struggles of the years 1832–1901. Once Chambers and Lyell, two geologists, had challenged the theological idea of a Creation in a single instant of time with their Uniformitarian thesis, Victorian England was quite literally cast adrift upon the seas of time. If the earth had been created not at some "still point" two billion years prior to the nineteenth century, as theologians had insisted, but was in fact the result of a continuing process of sedimentation that was still going on, then there was no effective escape from a continuing generation—not even in the illusion of *Genesis*. The impact of

From *Aspects of Alice: Lewis Carroll's Dreamchild as Seen through the Critics' Looking-Glasses, 1865–1971*, edited by Robert Phillips. © 1971 by the Vanguard Press.

the *Voyage of the Beagle* was not entirely dissimilar, since the concept of the fortuitous mutation implied a certain lack of any orderly progression from a Creation in the past. All those species on the Ark were not the boundaries of Divine Will, but rather a broad base from which creations were still taking place — some of which survived to replace their ancestors in the struggle for existence on earth. The menagerie that moves through *Alice's Adventures in Wonderland* clearly exists in a post-Darwinian tent, and new species can be called into existence merely by a mutation in the child's imagination or as a function of her size. They are the products of an anthropomorphic intelligence.

The child adrift in the city, as, for example, Dickens's Little Jo of *Bleak House* or someone perhaps slightly older, as Dorothea Brooke in George Eliot's *Middlemarch*, was a symbol for treating the effects of development and process in Victorian England. Having no surname, such children were the people without a past, not unlike those new species with whose generic Latin names Darwin busied himself. So many of the characters in nineteenth-century British novels are looking for origins, trying to locate a point from which they can date their existence. Casaubon, looking for the key to all mythologies, is perfectly suited to Dorothea Brooke because he is investigating historically what Dorothea Brooke is trying to live and what Tertius Lydgate is attempting to examine scientifically in his study of the origins of cell structure and their breakdown — particularly, to locate a point of human beginnings in an age that came to see all beginnings as merely another fiction in the saga of development. One way of "living" one's disconnectedness is to imagine existence itself as an alienated activity, and the child searching for foster parents is almost an *exemplum* of that psychic state.

Another manifestation of this same tendency is the effort of Victorian novelists to detach fictional activity in time. So often, novels are set prior to the occasion of their actual authorship: *Middlemarch* is removed from 1871–72 to the eve of the First Reform Bill (1832); Hardy's *The Mayor of Casterbridge*, set back to the years immediately following the passage of the First Reform Bill; and Meredith's *Diana of the Crossways*, set back from the 1880s to the 1840s, the period marked by a sequence of collapses wrought by speculation in rail shares. To make fiction so obviously historical has also an inverse effect: it makes history, and hence origins, a fiction.

The *Alice* books are no exception. Characteristically Victorian in his blurring of beginnings, Carroll, whose stuffy preference for perfection has made him an object of adoration to bibliophiles for a century, was apparently so unhappy with the first edition that the publication of *Alice's Adventures in Wonderland* was delayed until 1866. The tale itself was initially told at the famous boating party of three little girls and two British dons on July 4, 1862. That "golden afternoon," as described in Carroll's introductory poem, was actually, as we now know thanks to historical research, not so pastoral as its author would have us believe, but "wet and rather cool." But the mind that searches for a point of origins always hypostasizes it as pastoral and the pastoral mode seldom accommodates itself to the vagaries of British weather. The shower that had overtaken the group on an earlier expedition on June 17 obviously inspired the pool of tears. But the date specified in the story itself is precisely fixed at May 4, Alice Liddell's tenth birthday. Since the heroine of *Through the Looking-Glass* is seven and a half just six months later, her adventures should, were we dealing in historical reality rather than fiction, be dated at 1859 — the year Darwin shocked Victorian England by making its quest for origins an almost impossible task without the leap of faith. The significance of Alice's pursuit of time into a subterranean world beneath the layering of the earth's surface reverberates through the nineteenth century.

The predominating structure of the nineteenth-century novel, from *Mansfield Park* to *A Portrait of the Artist as a Young Man*, often seems to involve something like the Cinderella myth. Lionel Trilling's "young man from the provinces," whose growth and education is the subject matter of so many Victorian novels, is often a stray waif or wanderer who is rescued by being taken into one of those Victorian houses in the mode of Heathcliff, David Copperfield, or Bella Wilfer in *Our Mutual Friend*. The person who had been the object of the rescue then is miraculously transformed into a saint whose sacrificial gesture rescues others. And, as a reward, he is given rule of the castle or what is left of it after the Tories have been dispossessed. What is less clear is whether or not the transformed questor lives happily ever after. One suspects that such is part of the unfinished nature of every journey in the nineteenth century, and that the inheritor of Victorian spaces may turn out to be just as tyrannical as those who originally rescued him and set him to work. All those novels lent their names by houses — *Wuthering Heights, Waverly, Bleak House, Mansfield Park, Howards End*, to name just a few — have a way of being either domesticated into horrible middle-class apartments or degenerated into the whispering, echoing ghosts born from an incest with the past and manifested as the Gothic. If, indeed, this pattern is an inevitable feature of the novel in the nineteenth century, then the shift from Alice's journey in the *Adventures in Wonderland* to her posture in *Through the Looking-Glass* is more comprehensible: domestication within a veritable mansion of mirrors is the consequence of the search for meaning and identity. And Looking-Glass House is as much as part of the nineteenth century as the mirroring portraits that stare out at Dorian Gray and Stephen Daedalus at the conclusion of their respective labyrinthine journeys.

But to say all this is to say that the concept of the Victorian child marks a substantial shift from the eighteenth-century notion of childhood. That special status which had been afforded the child in *Emile* or Perrault's *Contes* seems to have been denied by the Victorians. As previously noted, so much mid-Victorian genre painting continues the tendency to be seen in the late eighteenth and early nineteenth centuries of clothing children in the garb of their elders. The judicial system, which had formerly placed the juvenile offender within a separate court system, now made the child subject to the workhouse and the prison. There are records of children in their teens being hung for petty crimes in the 1850s. Rather than attempting to protect children with special legislation, as the eighteenth century had done, the Victorian child was actually afforded the protection of minimum-hour and minimum-wage legislation *after* adults had already been awarded the same luxury. And, perhaps most significantly for the *Alice* books, Michel Foucault, in *Madness and Civilization*, argues that the nineteenth-century conception of a person judged insane appropriated the unfortunate individual to the status of childhood. Madness came to be regarded as a corollary of failed development, rather than a condition of animality, as it had been in the eighteenth century. This was yet another way of equating the child and the adult in the period; it meant no special protection, no *in loco parentis*, on the part of institutions. This transformation of the child, from infancy to adolescence, is nowhere better illustrated than in Hardy's *Jude the Obscure*, where a doomed infant is referred to as "Little *Father* [italics mine] Time."

To do away with childhood is, of course, to relieve parents of an important obligation; it makes every child an orphan in role whether he is in fact or not. And it means that every parent participates only vicariously in the upbringing of the child. To make every child a "little adult" has two disturbing effects: first, every adult participates in childhood fantasy freely, since there are no longer any barriers separating subject and object; and second, there is the threat of real damage to the family structure, since every individual's adaptation becomes a function of the conditions of his adoption. The orphaned child is, in effect, an exile not only from beginnings (and hence time, the dimension of *Alice's Adventures*), but family relationships (and hence space, the chess-board logistics of *Through the Looking-Glass*). This may well account for the amazing abundance of children's literature in the nineteenth century, which exceeds the output of any comparable period since the Middle Ages. What is denied in fact has a way of appearing in our fictional fantasy.

A quick reading of Froebel's *The Education of Human Nature* or Herbart's *Science of Education*, two popular books on the education of the child in Victorian England, reveals a sad burden. The role of the parents is minimized in the growth of the child because he is not seen to have an identity prior to the age of seven, the argument being that before that age, in Froebel's words, "the mind has not triumphed over the needs of the body." Twenty-five years later, Freud was first to suggest that such a triumph takes place only at an enormous cost and may not be one of the benevolent gifts of social evolution, but in fact may be a step backward—repression. One wonders whether Alice's attempt during her *Adventures* to constitute a social family among the animals is not the burden of Victorian exile. She is constantly attempting to discover her destiny by examining the will of each animal she encounters. It is as if to find out what was expected of her were crucial to defining her sense of self:

> "Well! What are you?" said the Pigeon. "I can see you're trying to invent something!"
>
> "I—I'm a little girl," said Alice, rather doubtfully, as she remembered the number of changes she had gone through, that day.
>
> "A likely story indeed! " said the Pigeon, in a tone of the deepest contempt.

Alice learns that few animals have wills as demanding and inflexible as those in the upper world of adults. Her identity is absolutely variable and conditioned by perspective rather than by the a priori demands of her governess. The resulting disorientation amounts to a dislocation that, from one point of view, is an individual fall; from another it is the whole world of humans that has fallen. The escape provided by the dream from the book being read her by her sister in chapter 1 of the *Adventures* leads to a world that, though dissimilar from the adult world above ground, quickly becomes filled with adult institutions, including obnoxious tea parties and trials. Wonderland is clearly no utopia, as a number of critics have insisted, but rather quickly assumes the same illogic and estrangement as the realm in which most humans exist. Petty jealousies and vindictive outbursts just as surely come to characterize the life of the garden, and there is little that Alice can do to prevent such an evolution. Although the first book has all the trappings of romance, including a quest for identity, a magic garden, magical transformations, and the luxuriance of perpetual springtime and a perpetual beginning, it ends with a trial, and there are no trials in utopias. It is strangely reminiscent of Carroll's experience upon seeing a sign that he thought read "Romancement," only to discover, upon getting closer, that it actually said "Roman cement." So much for what happens to romances!

To escape human willfulness, either deliberately, as in flight from one's past beginnings, or defensively, through the mask of boredom that provides a barrier to further brutalization, is always a worthy goal. But there is some real question about the success of such a venture. Even as Alice falls down the rabbit-hole, she seems to bear the burden of domestication, placing the marmalade jar in its appropriate compartment as if trying to maintain some vestige of order in a locale where disorder seems to be the rule. But the attempted flight from the effects of prior wills and commandments is perhaps, after the orphan, the most popular theme of Victorian verbal and visual art. So many of the orphans are bound by the testaments and codicils of guardians, which dictate the ward's potential marriage partner or the range of his occupation: Jarndyce *vs.* Jarndyce in *Bleak House*; old Featherstone's two wills in *Middlemarch*; the legacy of the title character in Trollope's novel *The Warden*; and Forster's linking of the inheritance of estates with the question of England's future. Clearly the will is, like so much vicarious participation in the nineteenth century, an effort to control destiny from another world beneath the surface. Those illustrations of deathbed scenes that grace the frontispieces of so many chapters in Victorian fiction and history are surely part of a last effort of the mortally ill to reconstruct a fictional family that he has created rather than had thrust upon him. And, similarly, Alice must learn that one escapes from one's familial past only temporarily, that the tedium imposed by the adult world is repeated among the children and their animals voluntarily as a way of establishing identities. Sadly, Alice discovers through the vehicle of the dream that the trial, or the reading of a will, or the determination of a guardian with which so much Victorian experience began, is a constantly repeated feature of human development. Her adventures end in the courtroom where mere whimsy determines guilt *after* sentence — which is to say that she concludes her journey at the same location from which so many nineteenth-century novels commence: a quite fortuitous and fictional judgment day. This might help to explain why Alice, while in Wonderland, is always attempting to discover how to *begin*, while simultaneously worried about how her dream is going to *end*:

> How she longed to get out of that dark hall, and wander about among those beds of bright flowers and those cool fountains, but she could not even get her head through the doorway; "and even if my head *would* go through," thought poor Alice, "it would be of very little use without my shoulders. Oh, how I wish I could shut up like a telescope! I think I could, if I only knew how to *begin*."

But on the very next page, the opposite concern is voiced:

> First, however, she waited for a few minutes to see if she was going to shrink any further: she felt a little nervous about this; "for it might *end*, you know," said Alice to herself, "in my going out altogether, like a candle. I wonder what I should be like then?" And she tried to fancy what the flame of a candle looks like after the candle is blown out, for she could not remember ever having seen such a thing.

Alice, like so many Victorian children, is initially aware of abandonment, of being trapped somewhere between *beginnings* and *endings* without the necessary map. She is a character in an epic with its defining time of *in medias res*, its catalogue of animals rather than ships, and its generic division into twelve books. And the first thing that Alice does is to cry, and then to talk to herself in soliloquy. It is that act, not the abrupt alterations in shape, which convinces the little girl that this realm is ruled by a double standard. The solitude of alienation induces a sudden transformation during which Alice becomes unsure whether she exists as subject or object:

> "Come, there's no use in crying like that!" said Alice to herself rather sharply. "I advise you to leave off this minute!" She generally gave herself very good advice (though she seldom followed it), and sometimes she scolded herself so severely as to bring tears into her eyes; and once she remembered trying to box her own ears for having cheated herself in a game of croquet she was playing against herself, for this curious child was very fond of pretending to be two people. "But it's no use now," thought poor Alice, "to pretend to be two people! Why, there is hardly enough of me left to make *one* respectable person!"

Alice's first response, then, is an act of self-reflectiveness, a recognition that a fall is also a *lapsus* in its ontological sense—a disintegration of the self into complementary components. She discovers that solitude is a short-lived condition, and the defensive posture that the self assumes is itself a mode of self-multiplication. What happens to Alice on the individual level is not substantially different from what takes place when she enters an estranged environment; sacred spaces quickly become filled up with animals and flowers that almost seem to be self-generating. She no sooner arrives in utopias than she humanizes them, and she humanizes them by introjecting her own schizoid-ness. It is a condition where convertibility and reversibility are norms: cats eat bats just as bats eat cats; punishment may precede the crime just as surely as following it; and the underground kingdom may parody the rules that govern conduct above Wonderland.

A large part of the "double-ness" that is a structural motif in *Adventures in Wonderland* and *Through the Looking-Glass* is a reflection of Alice's own condition, the result of a discovery that what she had thought to be a quest is but a metaquest, characterized by infinite regress and double-binds. John Fowles's suggestion in *The French Lieutenant's Woman* that *Dr. Jekyll and Mr. Hyde* is practically a psychological guidebook to Victorian England is surely applicable to Alice's quest. The romantic quest for communion with the alien "other" concludes when the self comes to the realization that the alien is but an extension of *it-self*. Hence, a journey that had previously been exterior is transformed into an interior quest upon the realization that outside and inside are the same—that the self (in this case, Alice) humanizes the other during the course of her adventures so that what had been Wonderland becomes a pretty socialized place after all. Hence two predominant patterns in *Alice* would appear related: the confusion between "self" and "other," and the fact that all of her solitary experiences inevitably end when she finds herself in the company of an extraordinary number of hosts. Everything from the pool of tears to the croquet game must be violated with something resembling overpopulation, the last effect of socialization.

One of the first things Alice learns in Wonderland is that punishment for transgression, a constant fear in the topside existence, is just as much a threat to her in the new environment. But rather than crying at the prospect of receiving physical punishment from those who lay down the law, she comes to understand that one is punished to stop the distress of previous punishment, not for any literal sins. Her own tears have resulted in the deep pool in which she finds herself, and yet she fears the further chastisement of being drowned in her own tears:

> "I wish I hadn't cried so much!" said Alice, as she swam about, trying to find her way out. "I shall be punished for it now, I suppose, by being drowned in my own tears!"

Like Dostoevsky's Underground Man, Alice discovers that retribution involves a scheme of ever-receding termini. In the spaces of Wonderland, one opens doors with keys only to find other doors. This multiplication is a replica of Victorian discipline couched in terms of a psychological domino theory; Froebel's somewhat bizarre development thesis imagined punishment as having a multiplier effect, so that the more swiftly the child is spanked or otherwise rebuked, the more effective is the punishment, since the guilty one feels doubly guilty about displaying tears and hence revealing how effective the initial retribution has been. Alice's education in the first of the two books is acquired as a direct consequence of guilt. Only when she offends one of the animals in this Victorian menagerie by a seemingly innocent expression of preferences, as when she mentions the cat to the mouse without the knowledge of the power politics of Underground, does she acquire knowledge. Carroll is actually making an astute observation on Victorian education, notably that the acquisition of knowledge and guilt over assumed transgression often accompany each other in nineteenth-century theories of development.

The real nineteenth-century fairy tale, from which *Adventures* and *Through the Looking-Glass* depart, had a conspicuously moral, if not didactic, purpose. Perhaps the tale that in plot most nearly resembles the *Alice* books is Christina Rossetti's *Speaking Likenesses* (1874). But that story has a remarkably unpleasant tone, designed to illustrate the evils of antisocial behavior. The heroine, a juvenile named Flora, ruins her own birthday party and, skulking away to pout in a yew-lined forest, finds a mysterious door leading to a great mirror-lined hall, where another party is in progress. Instead of ordinary guests, Flora sees the most grotesque children:

> One boy bristled with prickly quills like a porcupine, and raised or depressed them at pleasure; but he usually kept them pointed out-wards. Another, instead of being rounded like most people, was faceted at very sharp angles. A third caught in everything he came near, for he was hung round with hooks like fishhooks.

Flora is prevented from eating the delicious food by a domineering birth-day queen, and victimized by the other guests in a series of cruel games until finally she and they all build glass towers round themselves. Insults and missiles are hurled, and Flora awakes screaming, to find herself back in the yew alley. Throughout the dream, the moral is brought home with an almost repellent repetition. Since selfishness is the basis of Flora's naughtiness, Christina Rosetti makes each loathsome dreamchild exercise its own deformity for self-gratifica-tion. There is, for example, a typically Victorian game called Self Help, in which little Flora is ironed and goffered by Angles. Scarcely the equivalent of what Samuel Smiles talked about, this "game" would seem to be an illustration of the vices to which one is exposed in any self-gratifying activity. It is clear that the only way for the child to express her repressed sense of selfhood is by asserting herself, and the mode of assertion is mutual torment. And, like Carroll, Chris-tina Rossetti raises the problem of sequels on the last pages:

> And I think if she lives to be nine years old and gives another birth-day party, she is likely on that occasion to be even less like the birth-day queen of her troubled dream than was the Flora of eight years old; who, with dear friends and playmates, and pretty presents, yet scarcely knew how to bear a few trifling disappointments.

Speaking Likenesses illustrates two of the most characteristic features of nineteenth-century children's literature: the tendency to gloat over the physically grotesque, and a marked insistence upon the efficacy of punishment as *therapy*. If the mentally ill were regarded as children in the nineteenth century, there is also the sad hint that all misbehaving children were ill; Catherine Sinclair, in *Holiday House*, was to state this notion most succinctly: "Punishment is as sure to do us good when we are naughty as physic when we are ill."

Charles Kingsley, in *The Water Babies* (1863), was similarly interested in the educative value of punishment. The book is essentially one of the many ac-counts of a child learning to be good as he matures. Characteristically following the Cinderella pattern, Tom leaves the dark abode of the chimney sweeper's body and receives his education as a water baby in the sea under the stern rule of a Mrs. Bedonebyasyoudid. She holds weekly sessions chastising wrongdoers, on the principle of an eye for an eye. Since the punishment is a natural consequence of the sin, it always fits the crime. The real purpose of *The Water Babies* is to give an account of the education of the child from the waif to an honest English gentleman. But for Kingsley, systematic schooling was not the answer; it results in the kind of creatures Tom encounters on the Isle of Tomtoddies who have been turned into garden vegetables, "all heads and no bodies." Since a healthy mind must be balanced by a healthy body during this period of muscular Christianity, corporal punishment was seen to be as valuable as questions and problems. Tom's growth is related in three distinct stages: life in the river, where he is unconfined and allowed to exercise natural curiosity; then the period with the water babies, a time of painful moral training during which selfishness must be purged; and lastly, the journey to seek Mr. Grimes, during which the youth learns active goodness. It is this stage that perfects his character, that makes him fit for grace. In both Christina Rossetti's and Kingsley's stories, the plot line is linear, involving a pilgrimage from naughtiness to goodness, from transgression to redemption. But the final product is always a child that has become an adult, and hence is capable of retrospectively viewing and comprehending the meaning of the allegory.

Alice's Adventures in Wonderland, however, is a far more sophisticated volume that transcends the limitations of so much Victorian children's literature while at the same time posing new problems. Since many of the events are repeated *ad infinitum*, there is some question whether there is one experience rather than a series of hurdles. There would appear to be no progression in successive stages of maturity; even at the outset, Alice seems pretty grown up, taking great care to note location and to tidy up the pantry as she falls into the golden world. Since she continually repeats the same or similar mistakes (usually unwittingly insulting some animal by referring to a predator or a predatory set of values), it could be said that Alice may not mature at all during the course of her explorations. Like most heroines in Victorian children's literature, hers is the problem of identity. Once thrust into a strange kingdom, a relativism of size and language forces her to be literally at sea, even when she has climbed out of the pool of tears. And as previously noted, the problem of identity is inextricably bound up with the difficulty of locating a point of origin. Her comment, "if I only knew how to begin," applies equally to aliens, orphans, people at the beginning of initiation rituals, and, of course, storytellers. The only things we really know for sure about Alice's past are that she has been bored by her sister's incessant reading, and that the reading diet has resembled, not just a little, the type of children's literature written by Rossetti, Kingsley, and Hood; and that her responses are initially colored by her victimization at the hands of their art:

> It was all very well to say "Drink me," but the wise little Alice was not going to do *that* in a hurry. "No, I'll look first," she said, "and see whether it's marked *'poison'* or not"; for she had read several nice little stories about children who had got burnt, and eaten up by wild beasts, and other unpleasant things, all because they would not remember the simple rules their friends had taught them.

Rather than typical children's literature, with its pattern of repressive violence, *Alice's Adventures* is a self-conscious response to the absence of self. It takes little psychology to understand the dynamics of introjection, that the child oppressed by such literature quickly identifies with the aggressor in order to avoid further violence. One suspects that this pattern may well be responsible for the disappearance of the concept of childhood during the nineteenth century that has been discussed before in more detail. Unfortunately, it is typically a process by which an excess of brutality is always reinforced when masochism becomes sadomasochism. The only way to escape violence is either to pretend to be bored or to adopt the identity of the "other," both of which have the effect of doing away with one's sense of one's own identity.

This may well account for the merging of two genres in mid-Victorian England: the Gothic horror tale and children's literature. If children become monsters in the manner in which I have suggested, then one mode of brutalization is as effective as the other. The most amazing feature of, say, Dickens's treatment of children, is how quickly they are transformed into monsters. Even Oliver Twist's surname forces the reader to appropriate the twisting condition normally associated with creatures more closely akin to the devil! One effect of this identification with evil adults as an act of protection is that the only way of approaching childhood is by way of the opposite of satanic monstrosities— namely, the golden world of an edenic wonderland whose pastoral dimension gives it the status of a primal scene. Like the Victorian use of wills and the rapid increase in the production of pornography in mid-Victorian England, however, that golden world is a place of vicarious participation, an acknowledgment that the more real world of childhood has disappeared. Empson's idea in "The Child as Swain," that Alice's experience amounts to a Fall, is an oversimplification; the Fall is an a priori condition of the *Alice* books, not a description of their action.

When Alice discovers that the Mouse has enemies, she asks for an account of his "history," by which she refers to the rodent's autobiography. What she gets, as promised, is "a long and sad tale" that is printed in the shape of a tail. And, confusing history and story, the Mouse in effect gives us the entire plot of

Adventures in Wonderland: It begins with a meeting in a house and concludes with litigation in a courtroom. Such is to say that Alice learns little experientially, and comes finally to distrust her senses altogether, since two different sets of standards govern the exterior world in Wonderland and the earth's surface. She does, however, gain knowledge from another kind of adventure, the aesthetic adventure. Her entire world underground comes to exist as a collage of stories: pigeons are saying "a likely *story* indeed"; the Caterpillar replies to Alice's puzzling question by giving her a rhymed account of the life of Father William that is the "story" of his own furry existence, only slightly transposed; and the Footman at the house of the Duchess repeats his remarks "with variations." Yet, when Alice is asked to give an account of her own life during the Mad Tea Party, she is unable to oblige her curious hosts:

> "Suppose we change the subject," the March Hare interrupted, yawning. "I'm getting tired of this. I vote the young lady tells us a story."
>
> "I'm afraid I don't know one," said Alice, rather alarmed at the proposal.
>
> "Then the Dormouse shall!" they both cried. "Wake up, Dormouse!" And they pinched it on both sides at once.

All along, Alice learns that she must acquire an aesthetic sensibility, and somewhat self-consciously recognizes that she must become an artist in order to share her life with animals. Only when she makes public the private soliloquy of the first chapter can she distance herself from the confinement of corrupted utopias. One of the accomplishments of art is the idyllic transformation of the past, whatever one's present perspective may be:

> "It was much pleasanter at home," thought poor Alice, "when one wasn't always growing larger and smaller, and being ordered about by mice and rabbits. I almost wish I hadn't gone down that rabbit-hole—and yet—and yet—it's rather curious, you know, this sort of life! I do wonder what *can* have happened to me! When I used to read fairy tales, I fancied that kind of thing never happened, and now here I am in the middle of one! There ought to be a book written about me, that there ought! And when I grow up, I'll write one —but I'm grown up now," she added in a sorrowful tone: "at least there's no room to grow up any more *here*."

Alice must become an artist, transforming the outer or "green world" into the enclosed, autotelic pleasure dome of *Through the Looking-Glass*. Haigha and Hatta of *Looking-Glass* are clearly the Hare and the Hatter that had previously resided in Wonderland. The latter story takes place indoors in autumn; its predecessor, characteristically, takes place outdoors in the spring. And Alice is able to dissolve the looking glass for herself and her kitten with the hypnotic formula: "Let's pretend." Never was there such contrived artifice in *Alice*. In the first book, the reader is more interested in Alice's adventures, in what happens to her on a relatively experiential level. On the second trip, we tend to accept her and to look around with her, as if we were in that other transformed nature in Victorian England, the Crystal Palace. The excursion has moved from time to space, from an impressionistic, almost fortuitous cluster of events that seem unique to a more static outlook. In *Through the Looking-Glass* the somewhat arbitrary preferences of the geometrician who laid out the landscape and manipulates the chessmen loom large. As Harry Levin has wisely observed, the events of the second kingdom, like that of most attempts to transform the natural world, are given the dimension of something that has happened before and will happen again and again. Tweedledum and Tweedledee will fight; the Lion and the Unicorn will be ridden out of town; and Humpty Dumpty will continue to reenact his disappearing *act*. But, most importantly, we are aware that his movements are an "act," a dramatization of what has gone before. The garden in Wonderland is more like that tended by Keats's gardener, Fancy, who, in "Ode to Psyche,"

> e'er could feign,
> Who breeding flowers, will never breed the same.

Alice's Adventures in Wonderland stands to *Through the Looking-Glass* as play stands to artifice. The flowers in *Through the Looking-Glass* appear to be magic plants precisely because that is the only way by which the adult can enter the child's world. The two volumes are by no means the same book, and the fact that so many critics treat them as identities just illustrates one of the things Alice must learn—that primitive experiences do not have sequels except as vicarious modes of participation. At the conclusion of *Adventures in Wonderland*, Alice Liddell's sister, Lorina, also falls asleep—and dreams. And that vision is the vision of her younger sister having become an artist:

> Lastly, she pictured to herself how this same little sister of hers would, in the after-time, be herself a grown woman; and how she would keep, through all her riper years, the simple and loving heart of her childhood; and how she would gather about her other little children, and make their eyes bright and eager with many a strange tale, perhaps even with the dream of Wonderland of long ago.

This is a child who participates in the dream of her sister having become an artist, and by retelling the tale of Wonderland, democratizes and domesticates the experience of the kingdom. That tale which Alice tells is quite clearly *Through the Looking-Glass*, where, at the trial, the entrapment and attempted confession of growing up become, in the adult space, a chess game. Although there is a connection between the two (both represent the arrested movement symbolized in the word "checkmate"), games are the sequels of experience, an attempt to pattern the random, spontaneous movement of earlier adventures.

Like so many children, then, Alice begins her adventures in response to the brutality of the children's fairy tale only to become herself the teller of the story to the next generation. Like so much of the language in the two books, that motif is itself tautological. But the fairyland has suffered in the transformation, for it now can be approached only as "once upon a time," not, as in *Adventures in Wonderland*, by following the time rabbit! It is a transformation similar to the larger patterns operative in nineteenth-century literature as a whole. If the period begins with the image of a child in prison, it concludes with the adolescent having improved nature by turning his mind to unnatural arts. St. Stephen commences his escape from the Daedalian labyrinth by opening his confession with the words, "Once upon a time, and a very good time it was." But as we read further in *A Portrait of the Artist as a Young Man*, we discover that Stephen's coming into consciousness is related self-reflexively; he has been told the tale of his origins by someone else. For "Once upon a time" does not exist *from within* the children's world, but only from the voyeuristic gaze of the adult storyteller who has become an artist, as the most convenient way of recapturing time past.

Wilde, Lang, Macdonald, and other *fin-de-siècle* dandies were each to testify to the disappearance of childhood by their interest not only in writing children's literature, but by actually living in the polymorphous perverse world of the presexually aware child. *Alice's Adventures in Wonderland* is a *Bildungsroman*, but *Through the Looking-Glass* is a *Künstlerroman*, a genre wherein the child's apprenticeship is now indistinguishable from his existence-as-art. But turning life into art is itself a kind of horror story. And the jaded dandy, Carroll included, resembles, not just a little, the bored child. In their themes and development, the *Alice* books are as encompassing of the Victorian period as the image of the Queen of the pack of playing cards, the Queen whose dispossessed children, scattered over the face of Europe, came back to haunt the future of England in the next generation just as surely as did Alice's story.

NINA AUERBACH

Alice and Wonderland: A Curious Child

"What—is—this?" he said at last.
"This is a child!" Haigha replied eagerly, coming in front of Alice to
introduce her . . . "We only found it today. It's as large as life, and
twice as natural!" "I always thought they were fabulous monsters!" said
the Unicorn. "Is it alive?"

For many of us Lewis Carroll's two *Alice* books may have provided the first glimpse into Victorian England. With their curious blend of literal-mindedness and dream, formal etiquette and the logic of insanity, they tell the adult reader a great deal about the Victorian mind. Alice herself, prim and earnest in pinafore and pumps, confronting a world out of control by looking for the rules and murmuring her lessons, stands as one image of the Victorian middle-class child. She sits in Tenniel's first illustration to *Through the Looking-Glass and What Alice Found There* in a snug, semi-foetal position, encircled by a protective armchair and encircling a plump kitten and a ball of yarn. She seems to be a beautiful child, but the position of her head makes her look as though she had no face. She muses dreamily on the snowstorm raging outside, part of a series of circles within circles, enclosures within enclosures, suggesting the self-containment of innocence and eternity.

Behind the purity of this design lie two Victorian domestic myths: Wordsworth's "seer blessed," the child fresh from the Imperial Palace and still washed by his continuing contact with "that immortal sea," and the pure woman Alice will become, preserving an oasis for God and order in a dim and tangled world.

From *Victorian Studies* 18, no. 1 (September 1973). © 1972 by the Trustees of Indiana University.

Even Victorians who did not share Lewis Carroll's phobia about the ugliness and
uncleanliness of little boys saw little girls as the purest members of a species of
questionable origin, combining as they did the inherent spirituality of child and
woman. Carroll's Alice seems sister to such famous figures as Dickens's Little
Nell and George Eliot's Eppie, who embody the poise of original innocence in a
fallen, sooty world.

Long after he transported Alice Liddell to Wonderland, Carroll himself
deified his dream-child's innocence in these terms:

> What wert thou, dream-Alice, in thy foster-father's eyes? How shall
> he picture thee? Loving, first, loving and gentle: loving as a dog (for-
> give the prosaic simile, but I know of no earthly love so pure and per-
> fect), and gentle as a fawn: . . . and lastly, curious—wildly
> curious, and with the eager enjoyment of Life that comes only in the
> happy hours of childhood, when all is new and fair, and when Sin
> and Sorrow are but names—empty words, signifying nothing!

From this Alice, it is only a step to Walter de la Mare's mystic icon, defined in
the following almost Shelleyan image: "She wends serenely on like a quiet moon
in a chequered sky. Apart, too, from an occasional Carrollian comment, the sole
medium of the stories is *her* pellucid consciousness."

But when Dodgson wrote in 1887 of his gentle dream-child, the real Alice
had receded into the distance of memory, where she had drowned in a pool of
tears along with Lewis Carroll, her interpreter and creator. The paean quoted
above stands at the end of a long series of progressive falsifications of Carroll's
first conception, beginning with Alice's pale, attenuated presence in *Through
the Looking-Glass*. For Lewis Carroll remembered what Charles Dodgson and
many later commentators did not, that while *Looking-Glass* may have been the
dream of the Red King, *Wonderland* is Alice's dream. Despite critical attempts
to psychoanalyze Charles Dodgson through the writings of Lewis Carroll, the
author of *Alice's Adventures in Wonderland* was too precise a logician and too
controlled an artist to confuse his own dream with that of his character. The
question "who dreamed it?" underlies all Carroll's dream tales, part of a per-
vasive Victorian quest for the origins of the self that culminates in the controlled
regression of Freudian analysis. There is no equivocation in Carroll's first *Alice*
book: the dainty child carries the threatening kingdom of Wonderland within
her. A closer look at the character of Alice may reveal new complexities in the
sentimentalized and attenuated Wordsworthianism many critics have assumed
she represents, and may deepen through examination of a single example our vision of that "fabulous monster," the Victorian child.

Lewis Carroll once wrote to a child that while he forgot the story of *Alice*, "I think it was about 'malice.'" Some Freudian critics would have us believe it was about phallus. Alice herself seems aware of the implications of her shifting name when at the beginning of her adventures she asks herself the question that will weave through her story:

> "I wonder if I've been changed in the night? Let me think: *was* I the same when I got up this morning? I almost think I can remember feeling a little different. But if I'm not the same, the next question is, 'Who in the world am I?' Ah, *that's* the great puzzle!"

Other little girls traveling through fantastic countries, such as George Macdonald's Princess Irene and L. Frank Baum's Dorothy Gale, ask repeatedly "*where* am I?" rather than "*who* am I?" Only Alice turns her eyes inward from the beginning, sensing that the mystery of her surroundings is the mystery of her identity.

Even the above-ground Alice speaks in two voices, like many Victorians other than Dodgson-Carroll:

> She generally gave herself very good advice, (though she very seldom followed it), and sometimes she scolded herself so severely as to bring tears into her eyes; and once she remembered trying to box her own ears for having cheated herself in a game of croquet she was playing against herself, for this curious child was very fond of pretending to be two people.

The pun on "curious" defines Alice's fluctuating personality. Her eagerness to know and to be right, her compulsive reciting of her lessons ("I'm sure I can't be Mabel, for I know all sorts of things") turn inside out into the bizarre anarchy of her dream country, as the lessons themselves turn inside out into strange and savage tales of animals eating each other. In both senses of the word, Alice becomes "curiouser and curiouser" as she moves more deeply into Wonderland; she is both the croquet game without rules and its violent arbiter, the Queen of Hearts. The sea that almost drowns her is composed of her own tears, and the dream that nearly obliterates her is composed of fragments of her own personality.

As Alice dissolves into her component parts to become Wonderland, so, if we examine the actual genesis of Carroll's dream-child, the bold outlines of Tenniel's famous drawing dissolve into four separate figures. First, there was the real Alice Liddell, a baby belle dame, it seems, who bewitched Ruskin as well as Dodgson. A small photograph of her concludes Carroll's manuscript of *Alice's Adventures under Ground*, the first draft of *Wonderland*. She is strikingly sensuous and otherworldly; her dark hair, bangs, and large inward-turned eyes give her face a haunting and a haunted quality which is missing from Tenniel's famous illustrations. Carroll's own illustrations for *Alice's Adventures under Ground* reproduce her eerieness perfectly. This Alice has a pre-Raphaelite langour and ambiguity about her which is reflected in the shifting colors of her hair. In some illustrations, she is indisputably brunette like Alice Liddell; in others, she is decidedly blonde like Tenniel's model Mary Hilton Badcock; and in still others, light from an unknown source hits her hair so that she seems to be both at once.

Mary Hilton Badcock has little of the dream child about her. She is blonde and pudgy, with squinting eyes, folded arms, and an intimidating frown. In Carroll's photograph of her, the famous starched pinafore and pumps appear for the first time — Alice Liddell seems to have been photographed in some sort of nightdress — and Mary moves easily into the clean, no-nonsense child of the Tenniel drawings. Austin Dobson wrote,

> Enchanting Alice! Black-and-white
> Has made your charm perenniel;
> And nought save "Chaos and old Night"
> Can part you now from Tenniel.

But a bit of research can dissolve what has been in some ways a misleading identification of Tenniel's Alice with Carroll's, obscuring some of the darker shadings of the latter. Carroll himself initiated the shift from the subtly disturbing Alice Liddell to the blonde and stolid Mary Badcock as "under ground" became the jollier-sounding "Wonderland," and the undiscovered country in his dream became a nursery classic.

The demure propriety of Tenniel's Alice may have led readers to see her role in *Alice's Adventures in Wonderland* as more passive than it is. Although her size changes seem arbitrary and terrifying, she in fact directs them; only in the final courtroom scene does she change size without first wishing to, and there, her sudden growth gives her the powr to break out of a dream that has become too dangerous. Most of Wonderland's savage songs come from Alice: the Caterpillar, Gryphon and Mock Turtle know that her cruel parodies of contemporary moralistic doggerel are "wrong from beginning to end." She is almost always threatening to the animals of Wonderland. As the Mouse and birds almost drown in her pool of tears, she eyes them with a strange hunger which suggests that of the *Looking-Glass* Walrus who weeps at the Oysters while devouring them behind his handkerchief. Her persistent allusions to her predatory cat

Dinah and to a "nice little dog, near our house," who "kills all the rats" finally drive the animals away, leaving Alice to wonder forlornly—and disingenuously—why nobody in Wonderland likes Dinah.

Dinah is a strange figure. She is the only above-ground character whom Alice mentions repeatedly, almost always in terms of her eating some smaller animal. She seems finally to function as a personification of Alice's own subtly cannibalistic hunger, as Fury in the Mouse's tale is personified as a dog. At one point, Alice fantasizes her own identity actually blending into Dinah's:

> "How queer it seems," Alice said to herself, "to be going messages for a rabbit! I suppose Dinah'll be sending me on messages next!" And she began fancying the sort of thing that would happen: " 'Miss Alice! Come here directly, and get ready for your walk!' 'Coming in a minute, nurse! But I've got to watch this mousehole till Dinah comes back, and see that the mouse doesn't get out.' "

While Dinah is always in a predatory attitude, most of the Wonderland animals are lugubrious victims; together, they encompass the two sides of animal nature that are in Alice as well. But as she falls down the rabbit-hole, Alice senses the complicity between eater and eaten, looking-glass versions of each other:

> "Dinah, my dear! I wish you were down here with me! There are no mice in the air, I'm afraid, but you might catch a bat, and that's very like a mouse, you know. But do cats eat bats, I wonder?" And here Alice began to get rather sleepy, and went on saying on to herself, in a dreamy sort of way, "Do cats eat bats? Do cats eat bats?" and sometimes, "Do bats eat cats?" for, you see, as she couldn't answer either question, it didn't matter which way she put it.

We are already halfway to the final banquet of *Looking-Glass*, in which the food comes alive and begins to eat the guests.

Even when Dinah is not mentioned, Alice's attitude toward the animals she encounters is often one of casual cruelty. It is a measure of Dodgson's ability to flatten out Carroll's material that the prefatory poem could describe Alice "in friendly chat with bird or beast," or that he would later see Alice as "loving as a dog . . . gentle as a fawn." She pities Bill the Lizard and kicks him up the chimney, a state of mind that again looks forward to that of the Pecksniffian Walrus in *Looking-Glass*. When she meets the Mock Turtle, the weeping embodiment of a good Victorian dinner, she restrains herself twice when he mentions lobsters, but then distorts Isaac Watt's "Sluggard" into a song about a *baked* lobster surrounded by hungry sharks. In its second stanza, a Panther shares a pie with an Owl who then becomes dessert, as Dodgson's good table

manners pass into typical Carrollian cannibalism. The more sinister and Darwin-
ian aspects of animal nature are introduced into Wonderland by the gentle
Alice, in part through projections of her hunger onto Dinah and the "nice little
dog" (she meets a "dear little puppy" after she has grown small and is afraid he
will eat her up) and in part through the semi-cannibalistic appetite her songs express. With the exception of the powerful Cheshire Cat, whom I shall discuss
below, most of the Wonderland animals stand in some danger of being ex-
ploited or eaten. The Dormouse is their prototype: he is fussy and cantankerous,
with the nastiness of a self-aware victim, and he is stuffed into a teapot as the
Mock Turtle, sobbing out his own elegy, will be stuffed into a tureen.

Alice's courteously menacing relationship to these animals is more clearly
brought out in *Alice's Adventures under Ground*, in which she encounters only
animals until she meets the playing cards, who are lightly sketched-in versions of
their later counterparts. When expanding the manuscript for publication, Carroll
added the Frog Footman, Cook, Duchess, Pig-Baby, Cheshire Cat, Mad Hatter,
March Hare, and Dormouse, as well as making the Queen of Hearts a more fully
developed character than she was in the manuscript. In other words, all the
human or quasi-human characters were added in revision, and all develop
aspects of Alice that exist only under the surface of her dialogue. The Duchess's
household also turns inside out the domesticated Wordsworthian ideal: with
baby and pepper flung about indiscriminately, pastoral tranquillity is inverted
into a whirlwind of savage sexuality. The furious Cook embodies the equation
between eating and killing that underlies Alice's apparently innocent remarks
about Dinah. The violent Duchess's unctuous search for "the moral" of things
echoes Alice's own violence and search for "the rules." At the Mad Tea Party, the
Hatter extends Alice's "great interest in questions of eating and drinking" into
an insane *modus vivendi*; like Alice, the Hatter and the Duchess sing savage
songs about eating that embody the underside of Victorian literary treacle. The
Queen's croquet game magnifies Alice's own desire to cheat at croquet and to
punish herself violently for doing so. Its use of live animals may be a subtler extension of Alice's own desire to twist the animal kingdom to the absurd rules of
civilization, which seem to revolve largely around eating and being eaten. Alice
is able to appreciate the Queen's savagery so quickly because her size changes
have made her increasingly aware of who she, herself, is from the point of view
of a Caterpillar, a Mouse, a Pigeon, and, especially, a Cheshire Cat.

The Cheshire Cat, also a late addition to the book, is the only figure other
than Alice who encompasses all the others. William Empson discusses at length
the spiritual kinship between Alice and the Cat, the only creature in Wonderland whom she calls her "friend." Florence Becker Lennon refers to the Cheshire
Cat as "Dinah's dream-self," and we have noticed the subtle shift of identities

between Alice and Dinah throughout the story. The Cat shares Alice's equivocal placidity: "The Cat only grinned when it saw Alice. It looked goodnatured, she thought: still it had *very* long claws and a great many teeth, so she felt it ought to be treated with respect." The Cat is the only creature to make explicit the identification between Alice and the madness of Wonderland: "'we're all mad here. I'm mad. You're mad.' 'How do you know I'm mad?' said Alice. 'You must be,' said the Cat, 'or you wouldn't have come here.' Alice didn't think that proved it at all." Although Alice cannot accept it and closes into silence, the Cat's remark may be the answer she has been groping toward in her incessant question, "who am I?" As an alter ego, the Cat is wiser than Alice — and safer — because he is the only character in the book who is aware of his own madness. In his serene acceptance of the fury within and without, his total control over his appearance and disappearance, he almost suggests a post-analytic version of the puzzled Alice.

As Alice dissolves increasingly into Wonderland, so the Cat dissolves into his own head, and finally into his own grinning mouth. The core of Alice's nature, too, seems to lie in her mouth: the eating and drinking that direct her size changes and motivate much of her behavior, the songs and verses that pop out of her inadvertently, are all involved with things entering and leaving her mouth. Alice's first song introduces a sinister image of a grinning mouth. Our memory of the Crocodile's grin hovers over the later description of the Cat's "grin without a Cat," and colors our sense of Alice's infallible good manners:

> How cheerfully he seems to grin,
> How neatly spreads his claws,
> And welcomes little fishes in,
> With gently smiling jaws!

Walter de la Mare associates Alice with "a quiet moon" which is by implication a full moon. I think it is more appropriate to associate her with the grinning crescent that seems to follow her throughout her adventures, choosing to become visible only at particular moments, and teaching her the one lesson she must learn in order to arrive at a definition of who she is.

Martin Gardner pooh-poohs the "oral aggressions" psychoanalysts have found in Carroll's incessant focus on eating and drinking by reminding us of the simple fact that "small children are obsessed by eating, and like to read about it in their books." Maybe his commonsense approach is correct, but Lewis Carroll was concerned with nonsense, and throughout his life, he seems to have regarded eating with some horror. An early cartoon in *The Rectory Umbrella* depicts an emaciated family partaking raptly of a "homoeopathic meal" consisting of an ounce of bread, half a particle of beer, etc.; young Sophy, who is making a pig of herself, asks for another molecule. Throughout his life, Carroll was abstemious at meals, according to his nephew and first biographer, Stuart Dodgson Colling-wood: "the healthy appetites of his young friends filled him with wonder, and even with alarm." When he took one of his child-friends to another's house for a meal, he told the host: "Please *be careful*, because she eats a good deal too much." William Empson defines his attitude succinctly: "Dodgson was well-informed about foods, kept his old menus and was winetaster to the College; but ate very little, suspected the High Table of overeating, and would see no reason to deny that he connected overeating with other forms of sensuality." To the man who in *Sylvie and Bruno* would define EVIL as a looking-glass version of LIVE, "gently smiling jaws" held teeth which were to be regarded with alarm; they seemed to represent to him a private emblem of original sin, for which Alice as well as the Knave of Hearts is finally placed on trial.

When the Duchess's Cook abruptly barks out "Pig!" Alice thinks the word is meant for her, though it is the baby, another fragment of Alice's own nature, who dissolves into a pig. The Mock Turtle's lament for his future soupy self later blends tellingly into the summons for the trial: the lament of the eaten and the call to judgment melt together. When she arrives at the trial, the unregenerate Alice instantly eyes the tarts: "In the very middle of the court was a table, with a large dish of tarts upon it: they looked so good, that it made Alice quite hungry to look at them — 'I wish they'd get the trial done,' she thought, 'and hand round the refreshments!'" Her hunger links her to the hungry Knave who is be-ing sentenced: in typically ambiguous portmanteau fashion, Carroll makes the trial both a pre-Orwellian travesty of justice and an objective correlative of a real sense of sin. Like the dog Fury in the Mouse's tale, Alice takes all the parts. But unlike Fury, she is accused as well as accuser, melting into judge, jury, witness, and defendant; the person who boxes on the ears as well as the person who "cheats." Perhaps the final verdict would tell Alice who she is at last, but if it did, Wonderland would threaten to overwhelm her. Before it comes, she "grows"; the parts of her nature rush back together; combining the voices of vic-tim and accuser, she gives "a little scream, half of fright and half of anger," and wakes up.

Presented from the point of view of her older sister's sentimental pietism, the world to which Alice awakens seems far more dream-like and hazy than the sharp contours of Wonderland. Alice's lesson about her own identity has never been stated explicitly, for the stammerer Dodgson was able to talk freely only in his private language of puns and nonsense, but a Wonderland pigeon points us toward it:

"You're a serpent; and there's no use denying it. I suppose you'll be telling me next that you never tasted an egg!"

> "I have tasted eggs, certainly," said Alice, who was a very truthful child; "but little girls eat eggs quite as much as serpents do, you know."
>
> "I don't believe it," said the Pigeon, "but if they do, why, then they're a kind of serpent: that's all I can say."
>
> This was such a new idea to Alice, that she was quite silent for a minute or two.

Like so many of her silences throughout the book, Alice's silence here is charged with significance, reminding us again that an important technique in learning to read Carroll is our ability to interpret his private system of symbols and signals and to appreciate the many meanings of silence. In this scene, the golden child herself becomes the serpent in childhood's Eden. The eggs she eats suggest the woman she will become, the unconscious cannibalism involved in the very fact of eating and desire to eat, and finally, the charmed circle of childhood itself. Only in *Alice's Adventures in Wonderland* was Carroll able to fall all the way through the rabbit-hole to the point where top and bottom become one, bats and cats melt into each other, and the vessel of innocence and purity is also the source of inescapable corruption.

Alice's adventures in Wonderland foreshadow Lewis Carroll's subsequent literary career, which was a progressive dissolution into his component parts. Florence Becker Lennon defines well the schism that came with the later books: "Nothing in *Wonderland* parallels the complete severance of the Reds and Whites in *Through the Looking-Glass*. In *Sylvie and Bruno*, author and story have begun to disintegrate. The archness and sweetness of parts, the utter cruelty and loathsomeness of others, predict literal decomposition into his elements." The Alice of *Through the Looking-Glass*, which was published six years after *Wonderland*, represents still another Alice, Alice Raikes; the character is so thinned out that the vapid, passive Tenniel drawing is an adequate illustration of her. *Wonderland* ends with Alice playing all the parts in an ambiguous trial which concludes without a verdict. *Looking-Glass* begins with an unequivocal verdict: "One thing was certain, that the *white* kitten had nothing to do with it—it was the black kitten's fault entirely." Poor Dinah, relegated to the role of face-washer-in-the-background, has also dissolved into her component parts.

Throughout the books, the schism between Blacks (later Reds) and Whites is developed. Alice's greater innocence and passivity are stressed by her identification with Lily, the white pawn. The dominant metaphor of a chess game whose movements are determined by invisible players spreads her sense of helplessness and predestination over the book. The nursery rhymes of which most of the characters form a part also make their movements seem predestined; the characters in *Wonderland* tend more to create their own nursery rhymes. The question that weaves through the book is no longer "who am I?" but "which dreamed it?" If the story is the dream of the Red King (the sleeping embodiment of passion and masculinity), then Alice, the White Pawn (or pure female child) is exonerated from its violence, although in another sense, as she herself perceives, she is also in greater danger of extinction. Her increasing sweetness and innocence in the second book make her more ghost-like as well, and it is appropriate that more death jokes surround her in the second *Alice* book than in the first.

At Carroll's dream children became sweeter, his attitude toward animals became increasingly tormented and obsessive, as we can see in the hysterical antivivisection crusade of his later years. In one of his pamphlets, "Vivisection as a Sign of the Times," cruelty to animals, which in the first Alice was a casual instinct, becomes a synecdoche for the comprehensive sin of civilization:

> "But the thing cannot be!" cries some amiable reader, fresh from an interview with the most charming of men, a London physician. "What! Is it possible that one so gentle in manner, so full of noble sentiments, can be hardhearted? The very idea is an outrage to common sense!" And thus we are duped every day of our lives. Is it possible that that bank director, with his broad honest face, can be meditating a fraud? That the chairman of that meeting of shareholders, whose every tone has the ring of truth in it, can hold in his hand a "cooked" schedule of accounts? That my wine merchant, so outspoken, so confiding, can be supplying me with an adulterated article? That my schoolmaster, to whom I have entrusted my little boy, can starve or neglect him? How well I remember his words to the dear child when last we parted. "You are leaving your friends," he said, "but you will have a father in me, my dear, and a mother in Mrs. Squeers!" For all such rose-coloured dreams of the necessary immunity from human vices of educated men the facts in last week's *Spectator* have a terrible significance. "Trust no man further than you can see him," they seem to say. "Qui vult decipi, decipiatur."

"Gently smiling jaws" have spread themselves over England. The sweeping intensity of this jeremiad shares the vision, if not the eloquence, of Ruskin's later despairing works.

As the world becomes more comprehensively cruel, the Carrollian little girl evolves into the impossibly innocent Sylvie in *Sylvie and Bruno* and *Sylvie and Bruno Concluded*, who is more fairy or guardian angel than she is actual child. Here, the dream belongs not to Sylvie but to the strangely maimed narrator.

Any hint of wildness in Sylvie is siphoned off onto her mischievous little brother Bruno, whom she is always trying to tame as the first Alice boxed her own ears for cheating at croquet; and any real badness is further placed at one remove in the figure of the villainous Uggug, an obscenely fat child who finally turns into a porcupine. Uggug's metamorphosis recalls that of the Pig-Baby in *Wonderland*, but in the earlier book, the Cook let us know that Alice was also encompassed by the epithet—a terrible one in Carroll's private language—"Pig!"

Like Alice's, Sylvie's essential nature is revealed by her attitude toward animals. But while Alice's crocodile tears implicated her in original sin, Sylvie's tears prove her original innocence. In a key scene, the narrator tries to explain to her "innocent mind" the meaning of a hare killed in a haunt:

> "They hunt *foxes*," Sylvie said, thoughtfully. "And I think they *kill* them, too. Foxes are very fierce. I daresay men don't love them. Are hares fierce?"
>
> "No," I said. "A hare is a sweet, gentle, timid animal—almost as gentle as a lamb." [Apparently no vision of the snappish March Hare returned to haunt Lewis Carroll at this point.]
>
> "But, if men *love* hares, why—why—" her voice quivered, and her sweet eyes were brimming with tears.
>
> "I'm afraid they *don't* love them, dear child."
>
> "All *children* love them," Sylvie said. "All *ladies* love them."
>
> "I'm afraid even *ladies* go to hunt them, sometimes."
>
> Sylvie shuddered. "Oh, no, not *ladies!*" she earnestly pleaded. . . . In a hushed, solemn tone, with bowed head and clasped hands, she put her final question, "Does GOD love hares?"
>
> "Yes!" I said. "I'm *sure* He does. He loves every living thing. Even sinful *men*. How much more the animals, that cannot sin!" [Here the whole *Wonderland* gallery should have risen up in chorus against their creator!]
>
> "I don't know what 'sin' means," said Sylvie. And I didn't try to explain it.
>
> "Come, my child," I said, trying to lead her away. "Wish good-bye to the poor hare, and come and look for blackberries."
>
> "Good-bye, poor hare!" Sylvie obediently repeated, looking over her shoulder at it as we turned away. And then, all in a moment, her self-command gave way. Pulling her hand out of mine, she ran back to where the dead hare was lying, and flung herself down at its side in such an agony of grief I could hardly have believed possible in so young a child.

Sylvie's weeping over a dead hare is an unfortunate conclusion to Alice's initial underground leap after a live rabbit. Dodgson has been driven full circle here to embrace the pure little girl of Victorian convention, though he is ambivalent in this passage about "ladies." But his deterioration should be used as a yardstick to measure his achievement in the first of the *Alice* books, which a brief survey of some typical portraits of children in nineteenth-century literature may help us to appreciate.

Victorian concepts of the child tended to swing back and forth between extremes of original innocence and original sin; Rousseau and Calvin stood side by side in the nursery. Since actual children were the focus of such an extreme conflicts of attitudes, they tended to be a source of pain and embarrassment to adults, and were therefore told they should be "seen and not heard." Literature dealt more freely with children than life did, so adult conflicts about them were allowed to emerge more openly in books. As Jan Gordon puts it:

> The most amazing feature of, say, Dickens's treatment of children, is how quickly they are transformed into monsters. Even Oliver Twist's surname forces the reader to appreciate the twisting condition normally associated with creatures more closely akin to the devil! One effect of this identification with evil adults . . . is that the only way of approaching childhood is by way of the opposite of satanic monstrosities—namely, the golden world of an edenic wonderland whose pastoral dimension gives it the status of a primal scene.

In its continual quest for origins and sources of being, Victorian literature repeatedly explores the ambiguous figure of the child, in whom it attempts to resolve the contradictions it perceives much as *Sylvie and Bruno* does: by an extreme sexual division.

Little boys in Victorian literature tend to be allied to the animal, the Satanic, and the insane. For this reason, novels in which a boy is the central focus are usually novels of development, in which the boy evolves out of his inherent violence, "working out the brute" in an ascent to a higher spiritual plane. This tradition seems foreshadowed by the boy in Wordsworth's *Prelude*, whose complexity undercuts the many Victorian sentimentalizations about Wordsworth's children. The predatory child in the first two books, traveling through a dark landscape that seems composed largely of his own projected fears and desires, has in fact a great deal in common with Carroll's Alice. Carroll is truer than many of his contemporaries to the ambiguities of Wordsworth's children, but he goes beyond Wordsworth in making a little girl the focus of his vision. Wordsworth's little girls tend to be angelic, corrective figures who exist largely to soothe the turbulence of the male protagonists; his persona in the *Prelude* is finally led to his "spiritual eye" through the ministrations of an idealized, hovering Dorothy.

David Copperfield must also develop out of an uncontrolled animality that is close to madness—early in the novel, we learn of him that "he bites"—and he can do so only through the guidance of the ghostly Agnes, pointing ever upward. Dr. Arnold's Rugby, which reflected and conditioned many of the century's attitudes toward boys, was run on a similar evolutionary premise: the students were to develop out of the inherent wickedness of "boy nature" into the state of "Christian gentleman," a semi-divine warrior for the good. In the all-male society of Rugby, Dr. Arnold was forced to assume the traditionally female role of spiritual beacon, as the image of the Carlylean hero supplanted that of the ministering angel. Thomas Hughes's famous tale of Rugby, *Tom Brown's School Days*, solves this problem by making Tom's spiritual development spring from the influence of the feminized, debilitated young Arthur and his radiantly ethereal mother: only after their elaborate ministrations is the young man able to kneel by the Doctor's casket and worship the transfigured image of the-Doctor-as-God. Women and girls are necessary catalysts for the development of the hero out of his dangerously animal state to contact with the God within and without him.

Cast as they were in the role of emotional and spiritual catalysts, it is not surprising that girls who function as protagonists of Victorian literature are rarely allowed to develop: in its refusal to subject females to the evolutionary process, the Victorian novel takes a signficant step backward from one of its principle sources, the novels of Jane Austen. Even when they are interesting and "wicked," Victorian heroines tend to be static figures like Becky Sharp; when they are "good," their lack of development is an important factor in the Victorian reversal of Pope's sweeping denunciation—"most women have no characters at all"—into a cardinal virtue. Little girls in Victorian literature are rarely children, nor are they allowed to grow up. Instead, they exist largely as a diffusion of emotional and religious grace, representing "nothing but love," as Dodgson's Sylvie warbles. Florence Dombey in Dickens's *Dombey and Son* may stand as their paradigm. Representing as she does the saving grace of the daughter in a world dominated by the hard greed and acquisitiveness of men—the world that kills her tender brother Paul—Florence drifts through Mr. Dombey's house in a limbo of love throughout the book, waiting for her father to come to her. She ages, but never changes, existing less as a character than as a "spiritual repository into which Mr. Dombey must dip if he is to be saved." Dickens's Little Nell and Little Dorrit are equally timeless and faceless. Though both are in fact post-pubescent —Little Nell is fourteen, Little Dorrit, twenty-two—they combine the mythic purity and innocence of the little girl with the theoretical marriageability of the woman, diffusing an aura from a sphere separate from that of the other characters, a sphere of non-personal love without change.

Charlotte Brontë's Jane Eyre and George Eliot's Maggie Tulliver are two more sharply-etched little girls who grow into women, but even they represent, in an angrier and more impassioned way, "nothing but love." Neither develops in the course of her book, because neither needs to change: all both need is acceptance of the love they have to offer, which in Jane Eyre's case is fervently erotic and ethical, and in Maggie Tulliver's is passionately filial and engulfing. Both triumph at the end of their novels because they are allowed to redeem through their love the men they have chosen, who, as Victorian convention dictated, have undergone a process of development up to *them.* This reminds us once more that in Victorian literature, little boys were allowed, even encouraged, to partake of original sin; but little girls rarely were.

We return once more to the anomaly of Carroll's Alice, who explodes out of Wonderland hungry and unregenerate. By a subtle dramatization of Alice's attitude toward animals and toward the animal in herself, by his final resting on the symbol of her mouth, Carroll probed in all its complexity the underground world within the little girl's pinafore. The ambiguity of the concluding trial finally, and wisely, waives questions of original guilt or innocence. The ultimate effect of Alice's adventures implicates her, female child though she is, in the troubled human condition; most Victorians refused to grant women and children this respect. The sympathetic delicacy and precision with which Carroll traced the chaos of a little girl's psyche seems equalled and surpassed only later in such explorations as D. H. Lawrence's of the young Ursula Brangwen in *The Rainbow*, the chaos of whose growth encompasses her hunger for violence, sexuality, liberty, and beatitude. In the imaginative literature of its century, *Alice's Adventures in Wonderland* stands alone.

PETER HEATH

The Philosopher's Alice

A well-known story tells how Queen Victoria, charmed by *Alice in Wonderland*, expressed a desire to receive the author's next book, and was presented, in due course, with a loyally inscribed copy of *An Elementary Treatise on Determinants*. The tale is not true, unfortunately, and was formally contradicted long afterwards by the alleged donor himself. Yet it still dies hard, if only because it coincides all too neatly with the popular picture of Charles Dodgson, alias Lewis Carroll, as an eminent mathematician who wrote nonsense books for children. The sad fact is, however, that this story is no more true than the other. Whatever the world may choose to believe of him, the author of *Alice* was not an eminent mathematician, his books are not nonsense, and of all those who read them, it is children especially who have the smallest chance of understanding what they are about.

Carroll (or rather Dodgson) was indeed a mathematician, who taught the subject — drearily enough, by all accounts — to Christ Church undergraduates for a quarter of a century, and then gave up lecturing for good. An inveterate publisher of trifles, he was forever putting out pamphlets, papers, broadsheets, and books on mathematical topics, but they earned him no reputation beyond that of a crotchety, if sometimes amusing, controversialist, a compiler of puzzles and curiosities, and a busy yet ineffective reformer on elementary points of computation and instructional method. In the higher reaches of the subject he made no mark at all, and has left none since. Compared with such genuine eminences of the time as Cayley, Sylvester, or Henry Smith, to name only fellow-countrymen, Dodgson the mathematician is little better than a valley, and deserves no special interest or esteem.

From *The Philosopher's Alice.* © 1974 by Peter Heath. St. Martin's Press, 1974.

In the infant science of mathematical logic his place is a notch or two higher. He at least paid more attention to it than anyone else in Victorian Oxford, which is not saying much, and two short papers he published in *Mind* (in 1894 and 1895) toward the end of his life have a tiny corner in logical history, as do the diagrams he invented and made known in *The Game of Logic* (1886) and *Symbolic Logic*, part 1 (1896). The general effect of these works, however, is to show that on this subject also, Dodgson's outlook was provincial, even trivial, and somewhat behind that of his predecessors De Morgan and Boole, to say nothing of his contemporaries, Jevons, Venn, and C. S. Peirce. The one enduring legacy he has bequeathed to logicians is a large stock of entertaining examples, which are still regularly drawn upon, or unsuccessfully imitated, by writers of textbooks too modest or unimaginative to manufacture their own.

Dodgson's most interesting and original work in this line, although, strangely enough, it was never fully published, is an investigation of the mathematical theory of voting, which arose out of his discontent with the proceedings of electoral boards and other academic bodies in Oxford. Here he broke ground that has since been cultivated. With the recovery of his work by Duncan Black, he now enjoys, in one small area at least, the recognition due to a pioneer. But it is virtually certain that, without his extramathematical reputation to sustain them, few of his other professional writings would command the slightest attention today.

These facts, though unexciting, are of some importance. Dodgson, the drab exponent of dilemmas and determinants, has been so far overshadowed by the more colorful figure of Carroll, the theater-goer, photographer, gamesman, perennial pursuer of small girls, and creator of the best-known seven-year-old in literature, that it is easy to forget that they are one and the same man. It is equally easy to progress from this to the theory of Dodgson-Carroll as a schizophrenic author, whose two sides are unconnected with—even opposed to—each other. The Carroll persona then comes to be represented as a rebellious escapee from the tedious sobrieties of Dodgson, whereby all that the latter stands for in the way of Victorian orthodoxy is implicitly rejected and denied. Pleasingly romantic as it appears, such a view enforces an almost total misconception of what is best and most individual in Carroll's peculiar art. If *Alice* and his other writings in this vein are interpreted as a protest against the academic conventionality of his outward existence, the "nonsense" element in them is bound to seem an irrational or anti-rational product of a mind on holiday from the constraints of ordinary logic and ordinary life. If [my edition of *The Philosopher's Alice*] has any purpose at all, it is to demonstrate the exact opposite, namely that *Alice's Adventures in Wonderland* and *Through the Looking-Glass* are works of unsleeping rationality, whose frolics are governed throughout, not by a formal theory of any kind, but by close attention to logical principles, and by a sometimes surprising insight into abstract questions of philosophy. The earliest version of Alice's adventures may have been extemporized by Carroll on the famous boat-trip to Godstow; but all its more characteristic details, plus the whole of *Through the Looking-Glass*, were meticulously elaborated in Dodgson's study in Christ Church. Unless Carroll's work is also seen as Dodgson's, it sinks into mere entertainment; half its merits go unrecognized, and the nature and quality of its humor are thoroughly misunderstood. Once the identification is made, it soon becomes apparent not only why *Alice* is so much less boring than other writings for the same alleged age-group, but also why so many intellectual persons, not otherwise nostalgic for the nursery, should cherish and reread it from year to year. Their motive for doing so is the enjoyment of play, certainly; but it is play of a highly intelligent and not at all childish kind.

Carroll's fame as a nonsense-writer is by now so firmly established that it is probably too late to persuade anyone that, apart from a few isolated instances such as the Jabberwock poem, he is not strictly a writer of nonsense at all. The term "nonsense" is admittedly used imprecisely for anything that fails to make sense. But this may happen in more ways than one, and with very different results. Aristotle seems not to have considered the question, but if he had, he would almost certainly have held that the virtue of making sense is a mean between extremes: nonsense on the one hand, and absurdity on the other. The difference between the two is that whereas the former neglects or defies the ordinary conventions of logic, linguistic usage, motive, and behavior, the latter makes all too much of them. In these terms it is easy to see that Carroll stands at the opposite pole from the true nonsense-writer. Although as a literary category the term had not been invented in his day, his proper genre is that of the absurd. Instead of blithely departing from the rules, as the nonsense-writer does, the absurdist persists in adhering to them long after it has ceased to be sensible to do so, and regardless of the extravagances which thereby result. This is what Carroll and his characters habitually do. Their opinions, however ridiculous, are held on principle and backed by formal argument (often, of course, ill-grounded or fallacious), and consist, most typically, in extreme or perverse or ultra-literal-minded versions of idioms normally quite acceptable, or theories otherwise perfectly sane. The humor lies not in any arbitrary defiance of principle, but in seeing a reasonable position pushed or twisted by uncritical acceptance into a wholly unreasonable shape.

To enlarge for a moment on this contrast between nonsense and absurdity, it may be worth renewing the old and by now rather threadbare comparison between Carroll and his near contemporary Edward Lear. The comparison, indeed, is scarcely to be avoided; for when two undomesticated bachelors, both amateur and part-time authors writing (as they think) for the amusement of children, are an instant, permanent, and unparalleled success with a multitude of adults as well, it is not only natural to couple them, but irresistible to suppose that they must both have found an identical key to the same little door. On closer examination, however, the differences soon appear; in spite of their seeming likeness, there is not, after all, so very much in common between Lear, the itinerant landscape painter, and Carroll, the stay-at-home clerical don. The commentators find it surprising, for example, but it can scarcely be an accident, that though quite a few people shared an acquaintance with both of them, they were never brought together, and neither of them anywhere betrays the slightest awareness of the other's existence. Nor has it ever been shown that even such casual resemblances as do occur in their writings are the result either of borrowing, or the use of a common source. The most probable reason for this is that there was nothing to borrow. Their aims are divergent, and the means of achieving them almost entirely distinct.

Lear, for the most part, is a true nonsense-writer, who gets his effects by random aberration from a norm he does not respect. His nonsense, like his life, is essentially of a wayward and bohemian kind, and so far as it is more than merely the defensive expression of a melancholy temperament, is undertaken chiefly for the rebellious pleasure of irresponsible rule-breaking as such. Carroll makes a different point by the more insidious method of simply working to rule. Authority, as he sees it, is not there to be defied, or even seriously resented. The logical proprieties cannot be dispensed with, nor should they be, at least in waking life. Absurdity, the disgrace of reason, arises not from logic itself, but only when carelessness, obtuseness, or pedantry are permitted to usurp its mantle, to the confusion of common sense. It is unmistakably the abuses of logic, not its sovereign authority, that Carroll is concerned to repudiate, and its bungling practitioners whom he is anxious to correct.

The carefully regulated formality of Carroll's method enables him, unlike Lear, to construct an extended design. The quasimathematical patterns of cards and chess in the *Alice* books and their themes of size-change and mirror-reversal are only a part of this. Wonderland and the looking-glass world are closed universes, ruled by elaborate conventions of chivalry, with monarchs and nobilities and feudal retainers, courts of justice, duels, and ritual observances that recall the Middle Ages, though most of the trappings, from cucumber frames to railway carriages, come straight from Victorian England. Lear's world, if he can be said to have such a thing, is a great deal wider in extent, but by comparison a loose and anarchic place—a dafter Albania, say, or a wilder West, where nobody (except "they") is in charge, and where radical individualists and social misfits like the Dong or Uncle Arly are free to roam interminably on the hills, the Jumblies sail the seas, and well-nigh anyone is welcome to roost forever, if they wish to, on the Quangle-Wangle's hat. The Jumblies, too, take a marvelously random collection of baggage on their travels, and are wholly indifferent to where they are going or the safety of their vessel. Carroll's only comparable nomad, the White Knight, is as carefully equipped for emergencies as any Victorian tourist, though the needs foreseen are as unlikely as the precautions are exact.

In Lear, also, there is a persistent search for peace and happiness, to be achieved (as it is, for example, by the Owl and the Pussycat, the Duck and the Kangaroo, the Pelicans, and the Discobolus family) by settling down somewhere and doing nothing from then on. Carroll's two narratives are entirely free from such sentimental quests and yearnings. As Professor Empson has rightly discerned, their mood is essentially pastoral and picaresque. Alice is not looking for anything special in Wonderland, apart from the entry to the garden, and wanders at random or is passed from hand to hand by the inhabitants. In *Through the Looking-Glass* she is propelled by the Red Queen into a pilgrimage not of her own choosing, and sleepwalks through it to her final apotheosis as a Queen. But there is no evidence that she particularly wanted this, or greatly enjoys it when she gets there. Aims and ambitions play little part in the story, therefore. As a child and a dreamer, adventures happen to Alice, but she encounters them passively and cannot be said to seek them out.

Lear, furthermore, has no great cult of childhood, and does not employ the child's point of view. Carroll uses it throughout, partly because he is interested in how children think, but more because Alice as an embodiment of the *gesunde Menschenverstand*—the naive but not uncritical voice of common sense— enables him to telegraph his own departures from it, and to join the reader in protest at the excesses of *Vernunft* (reason), the overweening logical faculty of Humpty Dumpty and his peers, which persistently oversteps its appointed bounds, and ends, as any Kantian could have predicted, in antinomies, paralogisms, and paradoxes. Carroll is admittedly no Kant, and his books are no rival to the *Critique of Pure Reason*, but his underlying message is concerned, no less than the Critical Philosophy itself, with the bounds of sense and the limitations of reason. The form of the message is that of a *sottisier*: a horrendous catalog of philosophical blunders, logical fallacies, conceptual confusions, and linguistic breakdowns, which not only entertain but persistently tease the reader, compelling him to ask himself, "What has gone wrong here? Why won't this do?" and to find that it is not always perfectly easy to supply the answer. Lear's nonsense seldom makes use of such devices (the mouse-stuffing Bachelors, who sought out the wrong kind of sage, are a rare but notable exception) and in most hands they would soon become wearisome. Carroll's advantage, as a professional logician, is that he has an extensive repertory of tricks up his sleeve, and is very adroit at deploying them, often within the space of a single chapter, as variations on a particular theme.

Alice, although nominally the heroine and undoubtedly the central figure throughout, is in fact the chief butt and victim of most of the author's jokes, and is carefully prevented by her own earnestness from ever seeing them, or realizing the sources of her chronic confusion of mind. In this she resembles such other literary simpletons as Candide or Don Quixote, though she has of course no guide or follower to assist her, and combines in her own person both the stoic realism of Sancho Panza and the resilient optimism of Dr. Pangloss. Her apparent fortitude in traveling, Gulliver-like, alone through an alien society is tempered by the fact that she takes its strangeness almost entirely for granted, and reacts to it mainly with innocent politeness or mild astonishment, rather than revulsion or fear. Since she never actually encounters any serious danger, and is required to assert herself only in bringing the stories to an end, this attitude sees her through. She is not quite the heroine *sans peur et sans reproche* that certain commentators have made her. She talks too much, for one thing, is often snobbish, tactless, or imprudent, and tends to be rude to the lower orders. Nor is the author by any means blind to these faults; on the contrary, he is only too ready to draw attention to them, and here again there can be little doubt that his motives in doing so are didactic and practical, rather than aesthetic. Alice (the real life Alice for whom the adventures were written) was intended to recognize and blush for her failings, and to find in her fictional history not only a lesson in logic, but a sermon on morals as well.

Whether these excellent purposes were ever realized, there is now no need to conjecture; but the chances are that they were not. Alice very probably did what other children do when they are made to read about her, namely to get a fair measure of slightly bewildered fun from the narrative, and to miss the point of everything else. As a work of instruction and profit for the infant reader, *Alice* has never been anything less than a total failure. It is at once too difficult and insufficiently serious in tone for its deeper implications to come across. The same miscalculation, as it happens, has wholly prevented *The Game of Logic* from finding favor in the nursery. It has a board and colored counters, and purports to teach syllogisms to the young, but no sane parent is going to inflict on his family a recreation which, however, edifying, he soon finds tedious and barely intelligible even to himself; those who have attempted it have soon repented of their choice. Logic is a dry subject, even to undergraduates. Carroll had a genuine fondness for children, and up to a point, a genuine understanding of how their minds work, but he never had any hope of making little logicians of them, however artfully he might endeavor to sugar the pill, and there is no record that he has succeeded yet.

Alice's unfortunate miscarriage as a child's logic-book should not, however, be taken to imply that this aspect of the work is of no value, and that the world has been right to neglect it in favor of the more popular view of the piece as a mere farrago of amiable nonsense. Not only is it *not* nonsense, in the sense already described, it also contains, by implication, a great deal of excellent sense. The very defects that more or less rule it out as fit reading for children are precisely the qualities to recommend it to mature and intelligent adults. The notion that *Alice* is a grown-up book is certainly nothing new. Many readers find this out for themselves, and the fact has long been familiar to various sections of the academic world, including professional philosophers and logicians. Fiction, of course, is normally of no interest to philosophers — any more than facts are — but *Alice* is a book they can all understand, and many of them find it compulsive reading. Their habit, however, has been to keep this news to themselves, as if slightly ashamed of it, and to notify their addiction only by a growing propensity to quotation (dating from the early 1920s onward) and by the occasional insertion of a discreet article in a learned journal, remote from the vulgar gaze. Their interest in the matter has therefore largely remained unknown to the general public, which continues to enjoy *Alice* in its own fashion, without suspecting its true nature, and with no opportunity for discovering what lies behind its simple-seeming façade.

The results have been somewhat unfortunate. *Alice* has been left in the hands of literary critics and journalists, who until quite recently have been content to applaud its virtues in general terms, and have seldom examined it in depth. With few exceptions, the standard of earlier critical writing about the book and its author is depressingly low. Within this vacuum, both have been liable to fall prey to two classes of specialist interpreter, the allegorists and the psychoanalysts, who deserve some credit for attempting to dig below the surface, but whose efforts, for the most part have been more successful in adding to the literature of nonsense than in lighting a path to truth. The allegorists, in any case, are a self-canceling group, turning every one to his own way, and may be left to their anagrams and secret histories in the confidence that, until they are able to persuade one another, they deserve no hearing from anyone else. The analysts, after a determined attempt some years ago to take over *Alice* as a guide-book to the Dodgsonian unconscious, seem lately to have wearied of an unrewarding task; which is not to say that, in the hands of an Empson, for example, their approach is unable to add anything to a purely literary appraisal of the book.

The upshot of all this has been that, for want of accessible guidance to its logico-philosophical content, the ordinary adult reader of *Alice* has been left in the dark on matters essential to its understanding; matters which, though sometimes covert or technical, are yet in no way speculative or open to serious dispute. For the commission of logical error is normally a question, not of subjective interpretation, but of ascertainable fact. An invalid argument is invalid in any language and any possible world, and can not only be proved to be such, but may also, on occasion, be recognized intuitively even by those who make no pretension to a knowledge of formal logic. The general reader is thus often able to agree with Alice that "there's a mistake somewhere"; but further than that he cannot always go. If you don't know the principle that has been violated, or the name and nature of the mistake, then you don't know much, as the Duchess would say, and it might be worth knowing more. While [*The Philosopher's Alice*] does not offer to teach philosophy for nothing, or to spell out every single thing in words of one letter, it can at least claim to be the first full attempt at a serial — if not wholly serious — account of Alice's logico-philosophical misadventures in which she appears, for a change, in her true colors — no longer as the sweet little girl of tradition, but as a mind driven almost to the verge of unhingement by its encounter with the dark forces and mysterious taboos of language and thought.

EDMUND MILLER

The Sylvie and Bruno *Books* as *Victorian Novel*

The *Sylvie and Bruno* books together form Lewis Carroll's most ambitious literary work. Yet the general public is hardly aware of its existence. This is a great shame, for the work is more interesting and rewarding than it is generally given credit for being. While perhaps not a great work or an ideally conceived one, it contains many delightful examples of Carroll's brand of nonsense and is unique in the Carroll canon in that it consistently attempts to address an adult audience. The antiutopia of Outland, the charming escapism of Elfland (Fairyland), and the witty and significant talk of Elveston (England) are separately interesting. However, full appreciation and understanding of the *Sylvie and Bruno* books depends on seeing that they are based on a carefully articulated plan.

The volume titled *Sylvie and Bruno* was published in 1889, and *Sylvie and Bruno Concluded* was published in 1893. This publication history perhaps gives the impression that Carroll first wrote *Sylvie and Bruno*, that is, volume 1 of the full work, as a self-contained work and then produced a sequel four years later. But his own story of the writing is of a general assembling between 1885 and 1889 of substantially the whole of the two volumes. He had been gathering material with a book in view for many years; he claims to have done very little new writing when he came to put these pieces together. It was the great length of the completed manuscript that dictated the two-part publication. We know certainly that some of the illustrations that go with volume 2 were among the first illustrator Harry Furniss worked up in consultation with Carroll. The narrative is

From *Lewis Carroll Observed: A Collection of Unpublished Photographs, Drawings, Poetry and New Essays*, edited by Edward Guiliano. © 1976 by Edward Guiliano. Clarkson N. Potter, 1976.

continuous between the two volumes, and many incidents of volume 1 find their natural resolution in volume 2. Carroll has also developed an elaborate pattern of character parallels that unifies the work stylistically.

But I think it is worthwhile to make the point that volume 1 is not complete as it stands. Carroll describes it as having a "*sort* of conclusion," which he supposed had fooled all but one of his little girl friends when the volume was originally published by itself. But surely readers of ordinary sensibility would not think a work complete that ended without an overturning of the misrule of the Sub-Warden. And Arthur's sort of conclusion in deciding to set out for India is acceptable only in his personal history. The narrative needs a resolution of Lady Muriel's feelings as well. Yet at the end of volume 1 we feel very strongly that Lady Muriel cannot bear to hear Eric talk to her of love despite his official status as her fiancé: "But Lady Muriel heard him not: something had gone wrong with her glove, which entirely engrossed her attention" (vol. 1, chap. 22).

Carroll clearly intended us to have a single work in two volumes called *Sylvie and Bruno*. The diverse materials of this book are all rather neatly interwoven. There *are* minor discrepancies. Bruno, the son of the Elf king, should probably not report himself the servant of Oberon or say that he can sneak somebody into that king's hall because he knows one of the writers, as he does in "Bruno's Revenge" (vol. 1, chap. 15). And the Narrator should certainly not condescendingly address the reader as a Child, as he does suddenly in "Fairy-Sylvie" (vol. 1, chap. 14). But such discrepancies chiefly involve details in a number of self-contained early stories Carroll has incorporated, stories that inspired the longer work but are not always perfectly consistent with it. Discrepancies do not typically involve details of the English and Outlandish plot or the transition from volume 1 to volume 2.

II

The whole *Sylvie and Bruno* deserves special critical study of a structural sort. There are thematic implications to the elaborate method of storytelling Carroll has adopted. The great technical skill with which he manages the constant movement between dream and reality is generally acknowledged. But I think many readers are unhappy that Carroll chose so often to drift away from the nonsense of Outland and the antiutopia of Mein Herr's other world, and I do not think such readers have typically considered what is illustrated thematically by the very process of this constant movement from one kind of reality to another.

In the *Alice* books we may say that nonsense exists for its own sake. Perhaps one reason for the lesser popularity of *Sylvie and Bruno* is that Carroll was not content simply to copy himself in this genre, a point he makes in the Preface to volume 1. The *Alice* books have a structure of dream and a texture of nonsense. *Sylvie and Bruno* has the texture of dream itself. It presents dreaming, the various states of eeriness Carroll tabulates in the Preface to volume 2, much the way the *Alice* books presents nonsense. Nonsense may be said to have a higher order of logical consistency than ordinary reality. At least, the way nonsense works is by assuming a higher order of logical consistency than the complexities of our everyday language commonly allow. There *are* many and wonderful nonsense details in *Sylvie and Bruno*, but these have a different feel than the nonsense details of the *Alice* books. There often seems to be an insistent moral purpose to the *Sylvie and Bruno* nonsense. The *Alice* books are about another reality. In them dream has taken us outside normal reality to a place where we agree to suspend normal expectations. A new logic confronts us with its rigorous but alien consistencies. And we know we are dreaming. The plot is in fact resolved only by a waking up.

Sylvie and Bruno makes no simple leap to another reality. It concerns the borderline between dreaming and waking, but there is no confrontation. The first line of the dedicatory poem suggests a theme: "Is all our Life, then, but a dream . . . ?" We learn in the course of the work that the rigorous logic of nonsense is not so unreal after all. Of course, we also learn that the events of life work themselves out with unreal rightness in the end even in the "real" world. Normal expectations are shown to be underestimations of the power of love to influence events. A character such as Arthur Forester could not enter the world of either *Alice* without destroying the dream. The problem is that he is too logical. He operates in the same way that nonsense characters do, by taking problems to their logical extreme. But the problems are themselves real problems under real rules in his case. That is, the problems are real *moral* problems. And neither he nor Carroll questions the rules of Victorian Christianity under which moral decisions are to be made. In fact, Arthur often makes us go back and reexamine the full meaning of the rule. Through him we see the assumptions behind the normal expectations of our moral universe. He lectures us wittily on everything—and usually knows what he is talking about.

In a sense Carroll even finally chips away at our expectations of what nonsense itself should amount to. Bruno functions as a normal nonsense character. He is also logically consistent. But through him we see the assumptions behind the most normal things in our natural world, rather than as with Arthur in our moral universe. Bruno talks "real" nonsense. He is the one who can see "about a thousand and four" pigs in a field because, though he cannot be sure about the thousand, it is just the four he can be sure about (vol. 2, chap. 5). He is the one who can see "*nuffin!*" in the box of Black Light ("It were too dark!") because, as the Professor explains, that is exactly what the untrained eye would see (vol. 2, chap. 21).

Mein Herr, the Professor as he appears in the real-world scenes at Elveston, to some extent fuses nonsense and moral purpose. He might even be seen as returning the absolute consistencies of logic to the real world when he inevitably enters that world. On his planet they do everything the English way — but they go all the way. They try the two-party system, for example, not only in politics but in life, dividing their farmers and soldiers into teams of those who try to get the work done and those who try to prevent the others from doing it. Coming from the nonsense world of extreme logic and logical extremes, Mein Herr sometimes seems absurd to the characters of the real world who are incompletely educated to the moral purpose of the universe, as when Lady Muriel asks him to explain the curious experiments he participated in to try to improve dinner-party conversation. She, of course, thinks he is merely talking about "small-talk," but the whole point of the bizarre series of experiments is that people do not talk to each other enough about serious things. The real world needs the higher logic of Mein Herr just as it needs the invisible matchmaking of Sylvie and Bruno and the circle ruled by Sylvie's Jewel.

The logical nonsense of Mein Herr skirts the arbitrary abandon so appropriate to the two worlds of the *Alice* books by requiring us to think about the meaning of things in the real world. This is nicely shown in the incident of Fortunatus's Purse, an imaginative literary use by Carroll of the mathematical conception of the Klein bottle. We are familiar with the Möbius strip, a closed bank with a half-twist in it that has the peculiar property of being a single continuous surface with only one side. The Klein bottle is the extension of this conception to an additional dimension. It is a single continuous surface without inside or outside. Mein Herr suggests that Lady Muriel construct Fortunatus's Purse, a purse with all the world's riches in it, by sewing handkerchiefs together in a particular way. The first step is to make two handkerchiefs into a Möbius strip with a slit for the mouth of the purse. When Lady Muriel has done this, Mein Herr tells her that now all she has to do is sew a third handkerchief to the four exposed sides and she will have a purse of which the inside is continuous with the outside. Lady Muriel, having grasped the principle, puts the purse aside for final sewing up after tea (vol. 2, chap. 7). She is wise to do so, for the two-dimensional curiosity of the Möbius strip can assume a tangible physicality in our world, but the Klein bottle exists only in the fantasies of non-Euclidian geometers.

Mein Herr presents Lady Muriel and us with the conception of inside as outside. But Lady Muriel's discretion avoids a confrontation between logic and reality. Fortunatus's Purse both exists in the real world and does not. All the riches of the world are available to those who love. The task Carroll set for himself in *Sylvie and Bruno* was to sensitize his readers to this sort of hyper-reality. Fortunatus's Purse may be taken as an emblem of the theme of the work, that love is teachable and its power is boundless. We must learn to reach the depths of love contained in Fortunatus's Purse. And this love is all around us if we know how to look for it aright.

In the *Alice* books dream may be seen as an escape from our normal reality. Dream has a more psychologically sophisticated (or adult) function in *Sylvie and Bruno*. The Red God dreams a new game of creation, but the reader is quite awake through it all—or at least confident that he *can* awake to reality. But *Sylvie and Bruno* is contrived to make it much more difficult for the reader to maintain this sort of physical distance from the material. He drifts in and out of Fairyland with the Narrator. Thus he is gradually taught to understand that the limits of reality are blurred, that it is not so easy to say that this is the world of reality while that is the world of nonsense and fantasy. Ruth Berman has plausibly suggested that what she calls the dullness of the English scenes ("earnestness" would perhaps be more relevant and charitable) has a structural significance at least for the modern reader of the novel in making the Fairyland and particularly the Outland scenes seem more lively, more free, and finally more "real" in contrast.

Dreaming functions in *Sylvie and Bruno* as problem solving—as it often does in life. Dreams can restructure reality by omitting, changing, and adding details so that we can work out at least partial solutions to the continuing problems we have in the real world. This can sometimes be materially helpful, and it can often be psychologically helpful. In *Sylvie and Bruno* the characters of dream are vitally necessary to the solving of problems in the real world. Because they are, the work becomes a flux of reality and dream. It is no accident that here we find Carroll inventing the Time Machine (he is several years before Wells). An Outlandish Watch would be pointless in Wonderland because there we have lost all sense of what time it "really" is; the Mad Hatter's watch "doesn't tell what o'clock it is." But real time and eerie time exist simultaneously in the world of *Sylvie and Bruno*, and Carroll means for us to discover that neither is all there is. Reality is not enough; we need nonsense too. Drifting into a world of fantasy is not an escape from reality but a significant education about the nature of life. And reality is not an escape from nonsense. Our education goes on everywhere. Arthur teaches us most directly, but there are professors everywhere in this work (and college officers, the Warden and Sub-Warden). And it is only natural that the Narrator's dreams discover Bruno at his lessons, twiddling his eyes to see what letters do not spell, for example, and then seeing in EVIL only LIVE backwards (vol. 2, chap. 1). Eric Lindon learns the greatest lesson, that God answers prayer. This too is a lesson of love. And if we do not learn the lesson of love . . . why, we turn into porcupines.

III

That *Sylvie and Bruno* attempts to show the playful underside of a rather prim moral and religious view of reality, that it illustrates what we might call a leavening of reality with nonsense, has probably been understood by everyone who has read it. But the complementary point seems to have been equally important to Carroll, and perhaps too many readers come to the book from the *Alices* with fixed expectations. Do we want to hear that nonsense sometimes has to give place to reality, to a Carrollian reality of moral platitudes and sentimentality? And Carroll's moral view of reality does seem to be the source of our trouble. Side by side with his nonsense, Carroll presents an ostensibly real world whose values are sentimental and where events fall out according to the artifices of romance. The plot that animates and coordinates the two worlds is certainly a romance.

The genuine weaknesses of the novel for modern tastes all have to do with its nature as Victorian romance. There is, of course, a kind of general sentimentality to the whole treatment of love and religion. But there are also, admittedly, occasions when Carroll is rather more insistent than he should be even on his own terms if the book is to stand alone and actually demonstrate its theme of love and not simply proclaim it. An instance occurs when the Narrator has described Lady Muriel as "all that is good":

> "—and sweet," Arthur went on, "and pure, and self-denying, and truehearted, and—" he broke off hastily, as if he could not trust himself to say more on a subject so sacred and so precious. Silence followed: and I leaned back drowsily in my easy-chair, filled with bright and beautiful imaginings of Arthur and his lady-love, and of all the peace and happiness in store for them.   (vol. 1, chap. 6)

Most such sentimental excursions occur, however, in the fairy material. Somehow when Sylvie and Bruno pass through the Garden Door of Outland into the larger Fairyland beyond, Carroll seems to lose his sense of proportions and to give over his novelist's task of evoking emotional response. This is a common enough lapse for a Victorian novelist; Dickens lapses this way all too often. What is interesting is that in *Sylvie and Bruno* Carroll also on occasion manages to satirize what is conventionally sentimentalized. At one point Arthur is asked if he will not allow that someone is a sweet girl. He answers, "Oh, certainly. As sweet as *eau sucrée*, if you choose—and nearly as interesting!" (vol. 2, chap. 10). While there is much in Dickens that is not sentimental, I do not recall any incident that actually questions the sentimental system of values.

While we may not enjoy Carroll's Victorian sentimentality in this book, we can at least see that it is there for a definite purpose. This is a heavily moral book. It is a perennially difficult task for the writer to make his good characters interesting; Carroll has at least attempted to give some substantive life to his world of good. There is even a kind of narrative plausibility to his sentimentalizing of Sylvie. I find Sylvie the least rounded and least satisfactory of the main characters. The ending of the book could serve nicely as a *locus classicus* of Victorian sentimentality about feminine sweetness. The Narrator listens for a word from "Sylvie's sweet lips" but thinks that he hears instead "not Sylvie's but an angel's voice . . . whispering" (vol. 2, chap. 25). Yet is not such a characterization of Sylvie as angel better justified by the plot and theme of this book than, for example, the similar characterization of Agnes Wickfield in *David Copperfield?* Sylvie is in fact a supernatural being who exists to do good. The whole order of fairies exists in the book to show us in outline the workings of love. Sylvie's Jewel is merely the physical embodiment of a psychological truth for Carroll: "For I'm sure it is nothing but Love!" (vol. 2, chap. 19). The legend of the Jewel is both Sylvie will love all and all will love Sylvie (we cannot tell which) because to love is to be loved. The plot should be seen as a real attempt to demonstrate this point.

The sophisticated modern reader is almost bound to be unhappy with such a qualitative resolution of plot. He has nothing against love, but he would rather see it growing out of plot than magically justifying the most agreeable but unlikely developments. The resurrection of Arthur is like something out of Mrs. Radcliffe. But Carroll obviously did not see it that way. There is certainly a moral purpose behind his vision. And this sort of moral plot manipulation was a common feature of the Victorian novel. Carroll's contrivance is really rather clean and direct compared to the long-missing heirs and mistaken identities of Dickens.

But of course we do not usually come to *Sylvie and Bruno* from *Our Mutual Friend.* We come from the *Alice* books with the expectation of nonsense. And there is enough to reward our expectation so that we do not reshape it but rather find the book interesting in parts and not quite right. If we saw *Sylvie and Bruno* in its proper context as a Victorian novel, it would not be *Bleak House* or *Vanity Fair* or *The Egoist* because it is obviously not in the mainstream of novelistic development. But it does bear comparison, structurally, with *Wuthering Heights.* It is even more daring structurally. Both works are infused with the sentiments of the age and yet combine traditional materials in completely original ways.

And like the plot of *Wuthering Heights*, the plot of *Sylvie and Bruno* is pure romance. *Wuthering Heights* is a psychological study of the power of passion. But the conclusion of the plot, when it comes, is still a happy marriage that incidentally resolves the inheritance of two estates. *Sylvie and Bruno* ends with the conversion of the godless, the metamorphosis of the loveless, the resurrection of the good, and the reuniting of lovers. The complications that delay the righting of the universe in each novel also owe a lot to the tradition of romance. Romance multiplies improbabilities and coincidences to show the underlying neatness of a cosmic plan—exactly the way David Goldknopf has so astutely shown to be typical of the Victorian novel. Emily Brontë's young Cathy must symmetrically marry her cousins on both sides to resolve the passions of the senior generation, something the girl can only have the power to do because she was born into a family with such a neat genealogy. Carroll's Arthur must die to live—to live happily ever after with Lady Muriel in the knowledge that Eric has found God.

To say that *Sylvie and Bruno* is a romance in this sense means that it is a proof through narrative that reality has the moral purpose we wish it did. Such books exist to tell us what life cannot. To put the matter in the sharpest perspective, we may quote Miss Prism in *The Importance of Being Earnest:* "The good ended happily, and the bad unhappily. That is what Fiction means." Such a view of reality is implied by *Sylvie and Bruno*, implied structurally as well as thematically. The good do end happily, but the plot of the book exists almost exclusively for the morality. The characters are less important for themselves than because they illustrate the moral. Of course, the texture of the book, the texture of dream movement between Fairyland and the world of reality, often diverts us, sugarcoats the pill. But events are being manipulated to make a point about the way things should work out in the real world. That is the whole reason why things do happen in the book. And the fact that things do work out as they do is explicitly attributed to the power of a higher Providence than the Narrator's art. "I *know* that God answers prayer!" (vol. 1, chap. 25).

The test here is surely the supposed death and miraculous salvation of Arthur. We get to see Lady Muriel's faith bring her through the loss of her lover on their very wedding day. But then the high-comedy lovers get a second chance, and we know that when Arthur recovers they will have a perfect marriage of love. Of course the grave objection may be made to such a plot that reality seldom illustrates either perfect grief or happy marriage. This is, in substance, exactly the objection always made to romance (but it isn't true!). If we consider this manipulation of plot for moral purpose against the background of Victorian fiction, we see that Carroll is not only well within the limits of good form but also exercising considerable literary skill to keep the sentimentality in bounds. Arthur's death is handled with a good deal more restraint than the death of Barkis or of Paul Dombey, to pick places where Dickens succeeds beautifully in his gamble for our emotional commitment. The death of Mr. Dorrit's brother is such a muddle of sentimentality and abstraction that one is not even sure it is a death scene. The interminable death of Little Nell is, of course, the classic excess. In contrast, the supposed death of Carroll's Arthur is only inferred by the reader from a newspaper clipping. When it is presented to us, the clipping makes the event seem the properly cold and arbitrary work of fate. But in retrospect the newspaper format serves the more important function of justifying the misleading information. The Narrator did not commit himself to the death. Mistakes themselves are a kind of reality. The reader is tempted to complain that he has been cheated, but his complaints ring hollow in his own mind. We are tricked but not exactly lied to. Both the seeming death and the discovery are plausibly presented. The plan is out of fashion, but it is worked expertly. Even the Narrator's disgust when he believes that Lady Muriel has too hastily agreed to marry Eric after Arthur's death is worked expertly as narrative. We may cringe when he quotes *Hamlet* to himself, "The funeral baked meats did coldly furnish forth the marriage-tables" (vol. 2, chap. 25). But we also feel that the quotation as well as the sentiment is appropriate to the Narrator. His opinion *would be* both passionate and literary—and he would keep it to himself.

The whole romance structure of the work builds toward this religious validation of Arthur's supposed death. It is thus interesting that, in his notes on the drawings for *Sylvie and Bruno*, Carroll suggested Furniss draw Arthur as he would "King Arthur when he first met Guinevere." That the *event* is arbitrary is not a flaw but a consequence of the moral point proved by it, that love can work miracles. By the standards of moral contrivance in the Victorian novel it works very well. It is a good deal less surprising than Oliver Twist's genealogy or the blinding of Mr. Rochester or the ability of Tess of the d'Urbervilles to sleep through a sexual assault. The magic of Sylvie's Jewel simply works to tie the resurrection of Arthur to the various changes we have made and can make between eeriness and reality; it is one more transmigration from one world to another coexistent world. In this way Sylvie's Jewel performs its magic to make *Sylvie and Bruno* a single work structurally and a Victorian novel. This is in contrast to the *Alice* books, which share many elements of point of view with each other and some of these at times with *Sylvie and Bruno* but are contained by their separate dreams. The antiutopia of *Through the Looking-Gass* is very obviously structured within its dream of a chess problem. This chess problem is completely arbitrary and so does a wonderful job of organizing everything else in the nonsense book. In contrast, the incident of Arthur's resurrection is structurally arbitrary but demonstrates miraculously the morality expounded by its book. And so it is, in a high sense, the inevitable culmination of the plot.

IV

We might also profitably consider the sensibleness of *Sylvie and Bruno* as part of the Victorian character of moral earnestness. Of course nonsense is a variety of logic. But *Sylvie and Bruno* also contains a lot of serious talk well expressed, serious talk that might be called socially aware. Arthur is, for example, presenting a serious and worthwhile analysis when he argues that the introduction of small stakes in card games raises the whole moral tone of the enterprise by discouraging cheating (because we take all money matters seriously) and by consequently making what cheating does occur seem repugnant rather than amusing. He recommends the introduction of betting as a cure for the silliness of croquet matches (vol. 2, chap. 9). On a number of occasions Arthur calls our attention to the difficulties of making conventional moral judgments. Victories over equal temptations, he argues, can have very different effects for the world because of irrelevant differences in environment (vol. 2, chap. 8). "If we once begin to go back beyond the fact that the *present* owner of certain property came by it honestly, and to ask whether any previous owner, in past ages, got it by fraud, would any property be secure?" (vol. 2, chap. 3). Arthur is clearly Carroll's *raisonneur* despite the tentative disclaimer in the preface to volume 2, "I do *not* hold myself responsible for *any* of the opinions expressed by the characters in my book." Nevertheless, he cannot help remarking that he sometimes feels a great sympathy for one of Arthur's arguments. Carroll does not go so far with the aesthetic principle as more modern authors. And other characters sometimes speak with Arthur's voice of earnestness. It is the Earl, for example, who argues that we should take our pleasures quickly so that we can get more of them into life — though his suggestion of listening to music played at seven times its normal speed is perhaps not the most convincing conceivable (vol. 1, chap. 22). But Carroll's personality and thinking are clearly more a part of the personality of Arthur than they are of even the Narrator, the "Mister Sir" of Bruno, who is learning about the structure of life and so needs labels for everything.

It sometimes seems quite clear that Carroll's social conscience guided him in selecting many of the incidents for this work — a work Carroll says "had to grow out of the incidents, not the incidents out of the story." Carroll's concern with social causes is parallel to Dickens's. He is not against people who adopt causes. But he is very much against simple moral equations. This we see very clearly in the incident of the Anti-Teetotal Card, which says *That's where all the money comes from!* in answer to the Teetotal Card's *That's where all the money goes to!* Arthur's analogy of giving up sleeping to set an example for people who oversleep (vol. 2, chap. 9) shows us the importance of analyzing the problem of drinking to excess as a problem not of drink but of excess.

If anything, Carroll is too much in earnest. The particular suggestions made along the way in the work are often nonsense—betting on croquet matches, high-speed music appreciation, discontinuing overpricing at charity bazaars to cut down on moral self-satisfaction—are often nonsense or at least of no abiding importance. But the principles these suggestions force us to consider are always terribly in earnest and useful in helping us make ethical or moral discriminations. It is ironic that Carroll, who refused to play chess with bishops in nonsense books, should have felt it necessary in the preface to volume 2 of *Sylvie and Bruno* to answer the charge of having in the person of Arthur condemned most sermons as foolish (vol. 1, chap. 19). It is precisely because he was one of the few people wishing to take sermons seriously that he was able to have Arthur voice the complaint. Many preachers *do* misuse their privilege from interruption to talk twaddle. Again we may doubt that Carroll's solution—less frequent sermons—would answer to the problem now or would have answered to it in his own day. Unless we become, like the seventeenth century, an age that wants to learn from sermons and is perhaps even willing to pay lecturers for extra series in the evening, we are not likely to get good sermons no matter how infrequent.

Carroll's earnestness is one of the defining characteristics of *Sylvie and Bruno*. The fairy material may, in fact, even be seen as existing in the work only because of his earnest religious orientation. We have remarked Carroll's use of Victorian romance but we may go perhaps a step further and say that his specifically religious explanation of the workings of fate marks this work, despite its late date, as of the spirit of the *early* Victorian novel. Goldknopf has pointed out how a gradual reluctance develops in Dickens to attribute the fortuitous determinism of plot to God. By the time we reach Hardy, there is no God—or rather Hardy has taken over the work of God. And the direction of the modern novel has been to eliminate improbability and coincidence from plot because it no longer wants to give them the necessary moral justification. In *Sylvie and Bruno* Carroll has all the faith in coincidence of Charlotte Brontë. He knows that God orders our lives with love, and he humbly draws back from presuming to speak for God. Because he is a gentleman in religion, he creates the middle world of Fairyland to express the workings of fate. But we know his real characters are finally in the hands of God.

ALWIN L. BAUM

Carroll's Alices:
The Semiotics of Paradox

Time who sees all has found you out against your will.
— SOPHOCLES, *Oedipus the King*

When the Reverend Charles Lutwidge Dodgson was buried, in 1898, Lewis Carroll was set free behind the Looking Glass to continue his interminable game of chess with Alice, the heroine of his first two fairy tales, *Alice's Adventures in Wonderland* and *Through the Looking-Glass*. During the century since their game began, the Alice books have played to a larger reading audience than most traditional folktales. Even while Dodgson lived, *Wonderland* and *Looking-Glass* could be found alongside the bible on the top bookshelf of practically every Victorian nursery. Carroll's first biographer, Stuart Dodgson Collingwood, claims that the *Alice* books became primers for many Victorian children and that lines from them were cited in the daily press as often as lines from Shakespeare. If the popularity of the tales among children has since been eclipsed by cartoons manufactured in the television studio, the adventures have nevertheless maintained the status of cultural myth in the adult world. Much of that popularity is due to the sophisticated problems in physics, metaphysics, logic and semantics which surface during the course of Alice's wanderings. As fiction, the books have presented readers and critics with an equally formidable problem of decodification. The Duchess insists to Alice: "Everything's got a moral if only you can find it." Yet, attempts to sift a consistent frame of meaning from the texts have met with success as uncertain as the quest for a Boojum in Carroll's nonsense ballad, *The Hunting of the Snark*, and the course Carroll charts through the *Alices* uses the

From *American Imago* 34, no. 1 (Spring 1977). © 1977 by the Association for Applied Psychoanalysis, Inc.

same map employed by the Bellman to navigate the Snark expedition: "a perfect and absolute blank."

The author has also been an elusive quarry. Dodgson's affinity for young girls has prompted a number of attempts to exhume the spectre of unnatural desire from the texts. Like their folktale counterparts, Carroll's narratives abound in the imagery of sexual fantasy—rabbit-holes, magic potions which produce bodily metamorphoses, decapitation threats, desires to become a queen —yet the imagery itself is no more prolific than we would find in any fairy tale. If we accuse Carroll of aberrance in his fantasies, we would similarly have to charge human society, as collective author of the world's traditional literature, with neurosis or sensationalism.

The heterogeneity of approaches to Carroll's *Alices* is sanctioned by the overdetermination of semantic possibilities in the texts. Yet, there have been few attempts to discover a structural pattern in the narratives which would integrate various hermeneutic models. Perhaps it is just as well. The longevity of the tales is guaranteed by their enigmatic quality. The sense of the adventures is analogous to all of the "riddles with no answers" they contain: their aesthetic value lies in their insolubility. And if Alice were to find a solution either to the riddles or to her own motives for journeying into the imaginary world of unconscious possibility, the rationale for her nonsense adventures would go out like a candle. However, Carroll's fiction deserves critical attention precisely because it fails to offer solutions, a semantic context. It illustrates the importance of paradox in human language, generally, and the complex interrelations of the linguistic sign and its referent in symbolic discourse. Carroll's *Alices* have also played midwife to a genre of modernist fiction which has continued to nurture paradox. In this century, the narrative tradition from Joyce to Beckett, from Borges to John Barth, has taken Carroll's experiments in nonsense more seriously than Dodgson himself ever dreamed.

In form the Alice narratives most closely resemble traditional *Märchen* (Carroll himself called them fairy tales), except that they are explicitly framed in dream contexts. In authentic folktales the adventure cannot expose itself as a dream because its signifying function would be destroyed. The same is true for dreams. Only psychoanalysts may take them seriously as signifying systems. If the dreamer were conscious of his dream's significance, or even of the fact that it is "only a dream," he would not be "dreaming." The dream, like folktales and much modern absurd fiction, must put the hero's adventure in the context of lived experience. Any paradoxes or contradictions of physical law intrinsic to dream adventures must go unquestioned while the dream unravels. By the same logic, the nonsense of the dream experience must become apparent enough upon awakening so that a distinction between the two states of consciousness may be made (a function less absurd in non-literary experience than one might assume and one which is essential to signification in narrative structures). In fairy tales and dream fiction, the hero's acceptance of the impossible is not merely an ironic device, but it serves to indicate to the audience that the surrealistic episodes are meant to be understood metaphorically. Alice never questions the reality of the worlds underground and behind the looking glass; she even agrees to believe in the Unicorn if he will believe in her. As in actual dreams, it is her literal existence above-ground which is in question throughout the narratives. The absurdity of Alice's adventures points up the absurdity of waking experience (if only during the time of the dream). Although she protests that "one can't believe impossible things," she accepts the fact that she is speaking to an impossible White Queen who, when Alice's age, used to practice believing six impossible things before breakfast.

Like all fairy tale heroines and all dreamers, Alice must eventually awaken to discover that she has been "only dreaming." Yet even after the return to consciousness, Carroll forces the reader to believe one more impossible thing — Alice's sister redreams the Wonderland adventure exactly as Alice had dreamed it — a supreme paradox which characterizes the constant occlusion of boundaries between the two worlds. Similarly, behind the Looking Glass, Alice is presented with the dilemma of deciding whether she is part of the Red King's dream or he is part of hers. It is that old, insoluble paradox of idealist philosophy, one which continues to haunt Alice even after she awakens, since there are no grounds for proving that her return to consciousness is not also a part of the dream. Alice is, after all, "only a sort of thing" in Carroll's dream, one who would indeed be "nowhere," as Tweedledee remarks, if the dreamer left off dreaming. Carroll's interest in perpetuating the ambiguity is even more poignant in *Looking-Glass*, the sequel to *Wonderland*, which is full of shadows and sighs of nostalgia for Carroll's "infant patron," Alice Liddell, who had then reached the period in her life "where the stream and the river meet," as Dodgson characterized the boundary of pubescence when he customarily took leave of the young girls he had been visiting.

Carroll remarks in his diaries that the world of dreams seems as "lifelike" as the other, and he suggests that there is little basis for calling one reality and the other fiction. In conjunction with Carroll's observation, Martin Gardner notes the appropriateness of Plato's dialogue in which Thaetetus proposes to Socrates that it may be only the greater amount of time spent awake which leads us to favor waking experience as "true" and dreaming as "false." Carroll must have wondered what authenticity dreams might assume if the times were reversed. If daydreams were counted, the reversal might be an accomplished fact for most of us. Certainly Carroll makes a prime candidate for the role of the sleeping Red King since much of his own waking life was spent dreaming-up adventures and amusements for his child friends. Among these amusements was the first journey through Wonderland, composed *ex tempore* on one of Dodgson's excursions up the Isis river (from "Folly Bridge") with the Liddell children and Reverend Duckworth, and written down subsequently (as "Alice's Adventures under Ground") at the request of Alice. Thus Carroll's professed motive for the creation of his adventure into Wonderland was merely to entertain his child audience. However, in deference to the many readers who had attempted to make sense of his tales, Dodgson remarked in one of his last letters: "I'm very much afraid I didn't mean anything but nonsense! Still, you know, words mean more than we mean to express when we use them; so a whole book ought to mean a great deal more than the writer meant." Carroll is speaking of *The Hunting of the Snark*, but the suggestion is appropriate to the *Alices*. Equally appropriate is Caroll's confession, in response to requests to know whether *The Hunting of the Snark* were an allegory or a political satire, or whether it contained some hidden moral, that he frankly did not know.

It is plausible to discover certain latent meanings in Carroll's nonsense at various points in the narratives, but it is unreasonable to assume that he could have unwittingly composed a complete allegory. The Alice books provide the reader no consistent system of extratextual reference. As ingenious as some attempts have been to wrestle allegorical meanings from them—whether the reading is political, archetypal, or ecclesiastical—the systems have either fallen from their own weight, like a tower of Babel built out of a pack of Carrollian playing cards, or they have restricted severely the suggestiveness of the original. Shane Leslie's exegesis of *Alice in Wonderland* as a "secret history of the Oxford Movement" is a notorious example, although it is scarcely as zealous as Abraham Ettleson's "decodification" of the *Alices* as companion pieces to Judaic scripture. At the opposite hermetic pole are the many psychoanalytic studies which exploit the intra-uterine fantasies and castration complexes dominant in the work to demonstrate that Dodgson was arrested at the anal stage of development or that he labored all of his life under the oppressive shadow of an "infallible" father. Such readings do more justice to the ingenuity of their authors than they do to the genius of Carroll's nonsense, its power of suggestion. They appear as critical tours de force, moreover, because they assume that where there is fantasy there must be allegory, at least at the level of narrative content. Such interpretations press the sign into service as emblem, substituting a one-to-one correspondence between the signifier and the signified for a relation which normally is unbound in ordinary speech, and one which Carroll attempts to dissolve even further in his narratives.

Carroll was well aware of the essential arbitrariness in the relation between the linguistic sign and its referent long before Ferdinand de Saussure was to illustrate that such a principle is axiomatic to all language systems. One of the most obvious effects of Carroll's nonsense is to demonstrate the range of arbitrariness in the relation. The text of the *Alices* poses a problem of locating the linguistic context. It is similar to the dilemma faced by the Baker in his quest for the Snark: having left his name ashore, along with his portmanteau, the hero is obliged during the expedition to answer to any name, such as "Fry me," or, "Fritter my wig!" Through an exploration of ambiguities inherent in English, primary figurative expressions and homophones, and through neologisms and paralogisms of his own devising, Carroll develops a narrative code governed by the rationale of free association. The signifying axis of the text keeps reflecting upon its own ambiguities until those violations in the code become the rule. The linear development of the discourse is constantly interrupted (as was the first telling of the tale, through the importunity of the Liddell sisters) with the result that the rule of logical implication is cancelled out, and the "message value" (information) of the texts is nullified. The logos of the narratives is reflected in the Mad Hatter's riddle: "Why is a raven like a writing desk?" It is another insoluble conundrum, as Alice discovers later, yet an answer appropriate to the mood of the narratives would be: "Because they both begin with the letter *R*."

Elizabeth Sewell has remarked that the *Alices* are primarily commentaries on nonsense. More specifically, one could argue that they are metacommentaries on the nonsense of conventional English usage. Whatever consistent meaning attaches to the texts is less allegorical than it is metaphorical, or metalinguistic. *Wonderland* represents the underground of language, its literal self-reflection which is always present but disguised. Carroll examines chiefly those equivocal gaps in the code forced by an idiomatic *parole*, conventionalized poetic license whose ambiguities cannot be regulated by rule but only by precedent. The narratives serve to illustrate that "meaning is not an entity, but a relation," as Gilles Deleuze has suggested. But they carry the game a step further in allowing the signified to collapse into the signifier. Deleuze observes that in Carroll's nonsense "everything happens at the boundary of things and propositions," as in Chrysippus' remark: "When you say something, it comes out of your mouth; now, when you say *a chariot*, a chariot comes out of your mouth." In the same mood, the Duchess hurls the epithet, "Pig," at the infant she is nursing during Alice's visit; and, having received the baby as a gift from the Duchess, Alice discovers later as she carries it away that indeed it has become "neither more nor less than a pig."

On the other hand, such metamorphoses indicate that Carroll's nonsense is not *non sense*, that is, devoid of meaning. Merleau-Ponty has remarked that even the face of a dead man is condemned to express something. Certainly no utterance is *insignificant*; even silence has message value, as Alice's responses to the nonsense of her interlocutors indicate. Despite the apparent anarchy of words and things in the *Alices*, there is method evident in the madness. The pig's transmutation is actually a superb piece of logic, depending on one's point of view. Alice admits that as a child, her charge was "dreadfully ugly," but, she thinks, "It makes rather a handsome pig." And from Dodgson's point of view there was little distinction to be made between pigs and little boys, for whom, according to Collingwood, he had "an aversion almost amounting to terror." But there is a more profound implication in the episode which suggests that the word can become the thing. Language underground is not a process of classifying the physical universe, it is a means of creating a psychological universe. The inhabitants of Wonderland and the Looking Glass invert the Duchess's advice to "take care of the sense and let the sound take care of itself. " Invariably they force the sound to take care of the sense. Either the signifier swallows the signified, or the bond between them is severed, with the result that the sound image floats free to attach itself to any other sound with which it has the slightest association. "Did you say 'pig' or 'fig,' " asks the Cheshire Cat, after Alice has told him of her encounter with the Duchess. The question points out that the pig-baby is only a phonemic breath away from another metamorphosis; or that, from the Cat's point of view, the subject of Alice's anecdote is indifferently pig and fig at one and the same time.

The language spoken here is not the language of dream allegory but the language of real dreams. The major parameters of dream codification (according to Freud's model of the dreamwork) are also instrumental to the structure of Carroll's narratives. Freud observes for example that words are often treated in dreams as things. Thus when composite images are formed in dreams, as when a child might appear with an extended snout, or might grunt, like Alice's infant, the dream is creating a metaphoric association appropriate to its "deep-structure" or latent content. To Carroll, pigs, male infants, and figs are all fat and inarticulate, like the Uggug of *Sylvie and Bruno*, and thus indistinguishably distasteful (Dodgson was an ascetic vegetarian who despised overindulgence, apparently in all but story telling). The work of condensation in dreams is carried out also through portmanteau word formations (such as those in Carroll's "Jabberwocky"); through puns, verbal and visual (e.g., the "Mock" Turtle who is represented by Tenniel as part turtle, part calf); and through distortions of syntax, primarily teleological reversals which have the effect of making any expression equivalent to its converse. While free-falling down the rabbit-hole to Wonderland, Alice falls asleep pondering the question. " 'Do cats eat bats? Do cats eat bats?' and sometimes 'Do bats eat cats?' for, you see," the narrator explains, "as she couldn't answer either question, it didn't much matter which way she put it.

Other mechanisms of the dreamwork are equally apparent in the *Alices*. Freud suggests, for example, that logical relations in dreams are represented either through metaphorical constructs or through episodic sequences. In general, logical connections are reproduced in the form of simultaneity. One element juxtaposed with another is sufficient to indicate that they are associated in the dream thought. That is, of course the basic structure of metaphor. In dreams the composite is usually in images, as visual representation requires, although condensation may frequently appear in dream utterances. In the Alice narratives, the association is usually based on phonological and morphological affinities. Describing to Alice how he would get stuck in his sugar loaf helmet, the White Knight says, "I was as fast as—lightning, you know." Alice objects, "But that's a different kind of fastness." The Knight shakes his head and replies, "It was all kinds of fastness with me, I can assure you!"

Freud argues also that the "either—or" relation cannot exist in dreams. Whenever an alternative is presented within the dream, even when the terms are mutually exclusive, the relation may be read as one of conjunction. This is the basic structure of paradox, and much of Carroll's nonsense depends on it. "The Walrus and the Carpenter" begins with the sun and the moon jockeying for position over the sea, and concludes with a paradox of "acts versus intentions," as Gardner points out, in Alice's attempt to decide whether the Walrus is less culpable because "he was a *little* sorry for the poor oysters," or the Carpenter, because he ate fewer than the Walrus (who had sneaked some under his handkerchief), although Tweedledum observes that he nevertheless ate "as many as he could get."

The relative nature of judgments and definitions is argued similarly during Alice's first meeting with the Red Queen. In reply to the Queen's request to know where Alice has come from and where she is going, she says she has lost her way, only to be corrected by the Queen: "I don't know what you mean by *your* way . . . all the ways about here belong to *me*." Alice discovers soon after that those ways include the definition of words. The Queen has seen gardens for example compared with which the one they are in would be a wilderness, and hills which, by comparison, would make Alice call the one she is trying to climb a valley. "No, I shouldn't," said Alice, surprised into contradicting her at last: "a hill *ca'n't* be a valley, you know. That would be nonsense—." "You may call it 'nonsense' if you like," says the Queen, "but *I've* heard nonsense, compared with which that would be as sensible as a dictionary!"

In fact, the Queen's nonsense is not far removed from a dictionary which must define each of its lexemes in terms of others which in turn must be defined in terms of others, until, theoretically, each word would have to be used in its own definition. As a logician himself, Carroll was well aware of this essential semantic teleology in language, and he makes good use of it throughout the *Alices*. While the nursery rhyme about the Tweedle Brothers is running through Alice's mind, Tweedledum remarks: "I know what you're thinking about, but it isn't so, nohow." "Contrariwise," continues Tweedledee, "if it was so, it might be; and if it were so, it would be; but as it isn't, it ain't. That's logic." In Wonderland similarly the Duchess admonishes Alice: " 'Be what you would seem to be' — or, if you'd like it put more simply — 'Never imagine yourself not to be otherwise than what it might appear to others that what you were or might have been was not otherwise than what you had been would have appeared to them to be otherwise.' " Alice suggests quite sensibly that she might understand better the Duchess's moral if it were written down. In this case, of course, it would make little difference. The message reaches a threshold of vanishing returns in the course of its logical development and eventually cancels itself out. It is a paralogism similar to the classic "simple liar" paradox. For example, a card is presented which reads, "On the other side of this card is a true statement," and when the card is turned over, the message on it reads, "On the other side of this card is a false statement." Naturally, Carroll is aware of the pedagogical value of paradoxes for illustrating errors of reasoning to his students. The fundamental "error" of paradoxical propositions resides, of course, in the multiplicity of meanings which are forced to co-exist through an overdetermination of predication. When Carroll isn't reversing the order of syntax, or causing it to fork into mutually exclusive paths through a double entendre, he produces an interminable sequence of implication which nullifies the message. For example, "taking care of the sound and letting the sense take care of itself," the White Queen tests Alice's ability to do Looking Glass sums by asking her to add "one and one and one and one and one and one and one and one and one."

If syntax is a major problem for Alice, it implies also a problematic of time and space relations, since the propositional calculus serves to reinforce the interdependence of reason and a Newtonian universe in which all matter is identifiable in terms of its orderly relations in the space-time continuum. Thus the difficulty Alice has with the language code of her dreams is intimately bound to the problems she has with her existence in space and time. Her initial fall down the rabbit-hole, as Gardner observes, would have the effect, if the shaft went through the center of the earth, of keeping Alice forever in suspended animation. From that moment until she encounters the suspended enigma of the dreamer's identity behind the Looking Glass, Alice's self-image is continually called into question through paradoxes of logic or physical law.

Even the syntactic chain of narrative episodes is without rhyme or reason. Carroll admitted that he had originally sent Alice down the rabbit-hole without the least idea what was to happen to her afterward; and he contended that he pieced the narratives together from "bits and scraps," ideas that came to him "one by one at odd moments of reflection." Behind the Looking Glass Alice follows her moves systematically across the chessboard from pawn to queen, but the significance of the journey is less logical than it is metaphorical. Waking from the dream implies not only a return to the rules of consciousness, but it sets in motion, toward Alice's "coming-of-age," the hands of the intractable clock on the near side of the mirror. In the prefatory poem Carroll reminisces that Alice's crowning presages a "summons to unwelcome bed" of the "melancholy maiden" from whom he will ever be "half a life asunder." The distance between them, and the race it would take to bridge it, reminds one of so many of the races run in the narratives: the Caucus Race which has no real start or finish; the Mad Hatter's and March Hare's odyssey around the table in their hopeless race against "tea-time"; the White Queen and Alice racing to remain in the same square on the chessboard; Alice's futile attempts to catch the "motes" on the periphery of her vision—the things in the "Wool and Water" shop (including Humpty Dumpty in egg form) which move perversely to a different shelf when Alice focuses her attention upon them. Later, during her boat ride with the shop's proprietor (the Sheep who is the erstwhile White Queen), Alice tries to pick some "dream rushes" along the shore, the prettiest of which are always beyond her reach, while those she does gather melt away like snow in her hands. Gardner's suggestion that the rushes may symbolize Carroll's child friends is a compelling one. The episode underscores the problems Alice has throughout the narratives with "being and time." She exists in a Heideggerian universe which is created totally in the space between consciousness and the world, and which thus depends for its signification upon consciousness examining its own representational process. Alice's bodily metamorphoses in Wonderland are mirrored by the violations of spatio-temporal law behind the Looking Glass. Those violations are, of course, characteristic of fairy tales. They serve in part to sanction the fantasy that permits one to be any size one wants to be, as the Caterpillar intimates to Alice, or that permits him to be any place at any time he wishes. From the author's point of view, on the other hand, the violations of natural law and logic would allow Carroll to "hold fast" little Alice, as he puts it in the prefatory poem to *Looking-Glass*, with his "love gift of a fairy tale" by permitting him control over her size, age, and identity. After Alice tells Humpty Dumpty she is seven years and six months of age, he suggests that she might have done better to quit at seven. When she protests, "One can't help growing older," he remarks, "*One* can't, perhaps, but *two* can. With proper assistance you might have left off at seven." Quick to catch the implication, perhaps, Alice redirects the conversation, thinking to herself, that she had "had quite enough of the subject of age." Gardner and other commentators have drawn attention to the grim under-current of the adventures exemplified in these periodic "death jokes." Yet the implication of the jokes is only as serious as any child's desire to get control over time — to hold it in check and make it do his bidding, as the Mad Hatter and Carroll attempt to do.

It is reasonable to suppose that Carroll's fantasy reflects his concern to turn back his own clock. His argument with time continues throughout his work, to culminate in the "Outlandish Watch" of *Sylvie and Bruno* which, by analogy to the Looking Glass, reverses the order of events. Equally effective for the perpetuation of his relationship with Alice Liddell would be the attempt to hold her fairy tale surrogate in symbolic limbo. Throughout the narratives, therefore, Alice is suspended in the phenomenal moment, outside of time and space, and in continual ambivalence about her identity, until she eventually becomes "too big" for the dream, as she must, both literally and figuratively. While trapped inside the White Rabbit's house, Alice reflects:

> "It was much pleasanter at home . . . when one wasn't always growing larger and smaller, and being ordered about by mice and rabbits. I almost wish I hadn't come down that rabbit-hole — and yet — and yet — it's rather curious, you know, this sort of life! I do wonder what *can* have happened to me! When I used to read fairy tales, I fancied that kind of thing never happened, and now here I am in the middle of one! There ought to be a book written about me, that there ought! And when I grow up, I'll write one — but I'm grown up now . . . at least there's no room to grow up any more *here.*
>
> But then . . . shall I never get any older than I am now? That'll be a comfort, one way — never to be an old woman."

Such a pun on "growing up" indicates, moreover, where much of Alice's difficulties arise — in that problematical space between the literal and the figurative. Thus the existential dilemma Alice faces is bound up with the dialectical interrelation of the signifier and the signified.

At first glance, it seems hardly a flattering monument to Carroll's affection for Alice Liddell that her fairy tale persona should be put through the ordeal of playing pawn to an implacable semiotician. Alice eagerly exiles herself from the Empire only to find herself in a country which shamelessly abuses the Queen's English; and, as the champion of Victorian idiom, Alice is scarcely amused. She plays the role of adult *Pharmakos* caught up in a child's tangled web of free-association where the thing is continually sacrificed to the word and all words (and all things) are potentially analogous. Humpty Dumpty's defense of un-birthday logic concludes with the remark:

"There's glory for you!"

"I don't know what you mean by 'glory,'" Alice said.

Humpty Dumpty smiled contemptuously. "Of course you don't—till I tell you. I meant 'there's a nice knock-down argument for you.'"

"But 'glory' doesn't mean 'a nice knock-down argument,'" Alice objected.

"When *I* use a word," Humpty Dumpty said, in rather a scornful tone, "it means just what I choose it to mean—neither more nor less."

"The question is," said Alice, "whether you *can* make words mean so many different things."

"The question is," said Humpty Dumpty, "which is to be master—that's all."

The only response appropriate to such one-sided conversations is silence, and Alice is forever rendered speechless by her communicants. She persists, nevertheless, in her search for the code which governs dream communication. Even after waking from her Looking-Glass dream, when Alice tries to get an opinion on the adventure from her pet kitten, she finds problems with the rules governing dream discourse: "If they would only purr for 'yes,' and mew for 'no,' or any rule of that sort . . . so that one could keep up a conversation! But how *can* you talk with a person if they *always* say the same thing?" In response to Alice's request for clues the kitten only purrs, of course, and it is impossible for Alice to guess whether it meant "yes" or "no." Alice is similarly caught between affirmation and disconfirmation in her adventures. The space she occupies is mediate between the languages of the dream and waking life. Alice herself acts a catalyst to illustrate that the two languages are really interfused, whether one is awake or dreaming. She is like the sign itself, caught in the paradoxical space of the flame after the candle is blown out.

That space is objectified from the first moment in Wonderland when Alice is seized by the impulse to chase after the magic White Rabbit, to the last moment in Looking Glass, when Alice enlists her uncommunicative kitten's help in trying to decide who has been dreaming. Alice's initial fall is like the fall of man from a state of undifferentiated grace into a universe of hierarchical systems, constituted on a base of infinitely embedded oppositions, each of which requires a decision process for its articulation and its comprehension. In her free-fall through the rabbit-hole (which is lined, like Carroll's study, with bookshelves, maps, and pictures) Alice seizes a jar of orange marmalade. Finding it empty, she debates whether she should replace the jar on the shelf or drop it on the inhabitants below, the "Antipathies" she calls them, although "it didn't sound at all the right word." Her encounter with the marmalade, of course, contradicts the law of falling objects—she would have been unable to take the jar in the first place, and she could certainly neither replace it nor drop it, since she would be falling at the same rate of speed as the jar. It is one lesson in relativity among many in the books which look forward to Einstein's reduction of the distance between matter and energy. In the *Alices*, moreover, space and time are not only relative to each other but to language as well, an interdependence revealed, for example, in the decreasing number of hours spent by the Mock Turtle at his "lessens." Such punning follows on the heels of Achilles and the turtle in the paradoxical race proposed by Zeno of Elea where distance and time implode just a hair's breath from the finish line, or in the caucus race where the goal does not exist in space but in the time it takes to dry out. Outside of his narratives, Carroll was also preoccupied with the interrelation of laws governing language, space, and time. While Dodgson was defending Euclid's axiomatic approach to the world, in lectures considered by at least one of his students to be "as dull as ditchwater," Carroll was probing into space and discovering "black holes" everywhere. In his essay, "When does the Day Begin," we find him ready to race around the earth, clinging to the sun like Alice cleaves to her marmalade, in order to demonstrate just how relative human chronometry really is.

That Alice's dream friends go to non-Euclidean schools is further evidenced by the arrivals and departures of the Cheshire Cat. He goes so far as to tender his head to the Queen of Hearts minus a body from which to sever it, thus throwing the threat of decapitation (or castration) into a hopeless quibble over terms. The Cat himself could exist only as a figure-of-speech. To "grin like a Cheshire cat" was a current idiomatic expression even in Carroll's day. Alice corroborates her friend's low existential profile in her remark that she has seen a cat without a grin but never a grin without a cat. The Cat's grin is surely no more ubiquitous than that of Carroll himself, who delighted in hounding a pun until either the words or his child audience were exhausted. The Cat reveals also that Carroll's sorcery is sleight-of-hand sophistry. When Alice solicits advice which direction she ought to go, the Cheshire Cat replies:

> "That depends a good deal on where you want to get to."
> "I don't much care where—" said Alice.
> "Then it doesn't matter which way you go," said the Cat.
> "—so long as I get *somewhere*," Alice added as an explanation.
> "Oh you're sure to do that," said the Cat, "if you only walk long enough."

Alice's problem is that to get "somewhere" in her dream, she could never walk long enough. Just as one can never get "there" from "here" since, linguistically, *there* would become *here* once he arrived, so Alice discovers that *somewhere* is not located in the continuum of space and time but that of syntax-semantics.

Because language itself serves in large part to "locate" the speaker, to permit him to reaffirm that he continues exist, physically and psychologically, we might expect Alice's problems with directionality in her dreams to be mirrored also in her problems with the direction of discourse underground. During her free-fall to Wonderland, Alice tries to calculate the distance she has traversed in terms of the latitude and longitude she has gotten to, not that she has the slightest idea what those terms mean, the narrator reveals, "but she thought they were nice grand words to say." Like the Cheshire Cat, Alice exists in the interstitial space between physical and linguistic realities. It is a province again charted most accurately in *Hunting of the Snark* by the Bellman's map which dispenses with those "mercator's North Poles and Equators, Tropics, Zones, and Meridian Lines," since, "the Bellman would cry: and the crew would reply, 'They are merely conventional signs.'" In the Wonderland of dreams and fairy tales a blank map is ideal since it permits the traveller to take any route to his destination, or it allows him not to move at all, since he would be already where he wanted to go.

Traditional maps represent a semiotic system directed toward the pole of least syntactic ambiguity. If roads bifurcate and intersect, or if there are alternate routes to a certain city (there are no roads to "the country" which, like Wonderland, has no boundaries), those roads are clearly marked on the map, and all routes are discovered by the system (except the inconsequential footpaths). The map thus exhausts its semantic potential, since it assigns one value, consequently equal value, to each of its signs. Only the traveller (from the country) can create ambiguity in the system through his chronic hesitation between choosing the road which is straightest or that which promises some adventure, however slight. In Alice's search for adventure she finds herself continually at crossroads whose signposts reverse the order of things by reversing *l'ordre des mots*. The sign which points the way to the house of Tweedledee and that which directs Alice to the house of Tweedledum are mounted on the same post and point in the same direction. Signs which should have different referents keep turning Alice into the same semantic road whose signposts and milestones are puns, paradoxes, parodies, paralogisms, and portmanteau words, each of which switches the code from the axis of syntactic contiguity to the axis of semantic analogy, or paradigm. They are the same highway markers Freud discovered on the "royal road to the unconscious" in dreams (e. g., the processes of *condensation*, which forces two or more signifieds into one signifier, and *displacement*, in which one signified generates multiple signifiers), and in those mechanisms which produce the psychopathology of everyday life: parapraxis, paramnesia, and paraphasia.

In fact, the *Alices* could serve as guidebooks to the grammar which permits the unconscious to break through the "frozen sea of consciousness." The best model of both the dream-work and the structure of the *Alice* narratives is the "rebus" which Freud used to demonstrate the interchanges taking place between language and image in the formation of a manifest content (the signifier) appropriate to the articulation (symbolic cathexis) of the latent dream thoughts (the signified). Freud assumes that the primary function of the interfusion is to produce a representable (visual) content, but it is surely as much a question of "presentableness"; the dream-censor would best be circumvented by the diffusion of boundaries between word and thing. The signifier must be divorced from conventional meanings before it may be allowed to seek new reference, *mutatis mutandis*, in the semantic pool appropriate to the latent thoughts. The ultimate effect of these operations is the desocialization of the discourse. Humpty Dumpty reveals that substantives—nouns and adjectives—are very impressionable and easily manipulated while verbs are more recalcitrant. This is, of course, the case in language above ground; because the copula establishes the spatio-temporal link between subject and object, thus their relative identity (which is the only identity they have in the speech act), it is, as Humpty Dumpty says, the "proudest." Nevertheless, Humpty argues, "*I* can manage the whole lot of them! Impenetrability! That's what *I* say!" Whatever else Humpty himself may signify, surely he is very much Carroll, the master of nonsense, in this scene.

Carroll's investment in the impenetrability of a linguistic universe such as Humpty Dumpty describes is doubtless reflective not only of his role as poet and magician (where he began entertaining his sisters and younger brothers as a child), but of his desire to master language, particularly verbs, which at once served to represent the wall between himself and his young friends, and at the same time, one of his few sanctioned bonds with them. If Humpty Dumpty's language is inpenetrable to Alice, it is nevertheless not "his own invention," as the White Knight would say, despite the "extra wages" Humpty is willing to pay words to do his bidding. The language he describes is, on the contrary, ever *present* in waking life as the looking-glass reflection of social discourse—its alter ego, the subconscious. It is precisely the anarchy of association which social language must attempt to repress, since language is the primary vehicle through which pre-consciouis desire may articulate itself. Thus, social discourse zealously governs syntactic continuity, or diachronic expectation. The language of the pre-conscious is forced to ride under speech somewhat like Odysseus, clinging to the belly of a sheep, rides under the watchful eye (now blinded) of Polyphemus who would search him out and swallow him. Just as the guise assumed by Odysseus is that of "No-man," so in Carroll's adventures, Alice is in constant danger of losing her identity. The Queen of Hearts standing over her gardeners, trying to decide which among them is guilty of painting her white roses red when they all have their redundantly signifying backs turned toward her, is also a model of Cyclopean syntax—her response to everything is "Off with his head!" Happily, the queen would as likely recognize the discourse of this pre-conscious and to "suppress its evidence" as she would be able to cut off the head of the Cheshire Cat without his body being present. The view of language created here is one in which the signifier of consciousness is merely an excuse for the articulation of the latent signified—a view shared of course by Freud and by Carroll, if not by the Reverend Charles Dodgson.

In all archetypal struggles—whether social, oneiric, or mythical—the repressive process is marked by code "displacement," in the Freudian sense of the ego's creation of symbolic gratification for prohibited desire. In the *Alices* as in myth, the agonistic confrontation is foreordained through the prophetic word of the oracle because the contest is "fixed" beforehand—the goal is not to win but to *represent* the struggle itself since, like the two halves of the sign, neither desire nor social demand may ever be eliminated because each is covertly trying to accommodate its demands to the other. Thus the battle is as redundant as that between the "Lion and the Unicorn" or "Tweedledum and Tweedledee." Language itself is ultimately the arbiter, or mediator. Logical development of many episodes in the *Alice* books is prescribed in those oracular nursery rhymes which Alice repeats, almost as an incantatory formula, for calling into existence the creatures of her dreams. Like the Cheshire Cat, almost all of them owe their existence to language—Tweedledum and Tweedledee, Humpty Dumpty, the Mad Hatter and the March Hare, the King, Queen, and Knave of Hearts—all are literal incorporations of literary tropes or figurative expressions. Thus the confrontation of codes governing Alice's and her dream creatures' discourse is a parable doomed to the redundancy of expression found in the puns and paradoxes they articulate.

That redundance emphasizes the ritual nature of the narratives. If Alice is *pharmakos* it is because she too is doomed, (like Dionysus, the "twice-born," or anyone who stands midway between the world of consciousness and the unconscious) to recurrent *sparagmos*, in which the victim's words are torn asunder and scattered over the earth only to permit regeneration through a new synthesis. Carroll's dalliance with Alice's size and direction in the narratives is analogous to the sport he takes with her language. She becomes his *Spielzeug* in the archetypal game of *Fort! Da!* in which, according to Freud, through the ritual discarding and retrieving of an object the child gains some metaphorical control over his separation anxieties, or more generally, over the concepts of "presence" and "absence" so essential in their various forms to his physical and psychological survival. In the *Alices*, the threat posed by the protean language games is directed toward Alice's "syntagmatic" existence. Progression in the discourse is continually sacrificed to proliferation of choices which become available at each step in the spoken chain, a problem revealed in Alice's lament to her kitten that you can't talk to someone if they always say the same thing.

Coupled with her language problems, Alice finds it difficult to remember who she is. The Red Queen, who is fond of admonishing Alice to "Speak in French when you can't think of the English for a thing—turn out your toes as you walk—and remember who you are!" suggests also that Alice speak when she is spoken to. Alice protests that if the rule were strictly obeyed nobody would ever speak—it is one of the few debates which she wins. The implication is that speaking and being are interdependent. Alice finds that she is continually losing herself in the language of her dreams—most dramatically in the "Wood-where-things-have-no-names" where the boundaries between nature and culture are temporarily occluded solely through the loss of the nominal function of language. Symbolization of such boundary transgressions is characteristic of traditional literature. Through the deconstruction of the linguistic code which allows "predication" of the ego, the ritual infrastructure of this kind of discourse permits semantic overdetermination in the content, thus the metaphorical proliferation of identities.

The Cheshire Cat exploits Alice's manner of speaking to prove that she must be insane or she would not have come to Wonderland where everyone, as if by definition, is "quite mad." Alice suspects a tautology in the Cat's reasoning, but she finds herself enmeshed in its syllogistic network. The Cat would accept no contradictions, of course, even if Alice could find them—particularly those dependent upon the chronology of his utterance. Like the White Queen, he would see nothing anachronistic in taking as many as five days and five nights together—"for warmth"—she maintains, even though they would be five times as cold by the same logic. The Cat would concur also with the Queen's dismay over Alice's manner of thinking: "It's a poor sort of memory that only works backwards," she remarks. One advantage of "living backward" according to the Queen, is a memory which works "both ways." In strict observance of the rules of order behind the Looking Glass, one's memory should only work forward; but in that case, the reversal of directions would have little effect on the functional processing of experience into linear chains by memory. Once Alice had gotten used to living backward, a memory which worked to anticipate events would seem only natural in a world where events, as in a film running in reverse, were going the same direction. On the other hand, a memory such as the one described by the Queen would be no "memory" at all unless, of course, it worked forward and backward at will. Anyone who enjoyed the dubious gift of the Queen's memory would either suffer the phenomenological shock of total recall and projection, and would have to take to his bed, as the hero does in Jorge Luis Borges's short story, "Funes, the Memorious"; or, he would suffer perpetual amnesia, each moment of his existence would demand a new phenomenal self. While such a memory would prove inexpedient to physical survival, it is a fantasy frequently projected in myth as the chief attribute which separates mortals from immortals.

When threatened, Alice tries to recover her identity by appealing to her own poor excuse for a memory. On those occasions she discovers that the "words did not come the same as they used to do," a consequence of being in a metaphorical world, and each attempt to remember ends in a parody of the systems that governed her former life; below ground she finds the syntax has remained the same while the content is completely changed. Parody depends upon the occluding of the decision process which ordinarily permits distinction between two speech acts. While the code remains constant there is again a proliferation of possible contents which, theoretically, could go on forever. Like puns, parody exemplifies the irony that the progressive dimension of signification is only an illusion of syntactic chaining which masks the ultimate redundancy of those contents. It is a pardox similar to that of man's development of a system for measuring his progress in linear time based upon the endless revolutions of stellar bodies around each other in absolute space. Like all heroes of myth and dreams, Alice must only suffer the ordeal of relativity in space-time in order to realize phantasized psychological selves. After tasting the magic cakes marked "Eat me!" she attempts to measure how much she has grown by placing her hand on top of her head, "quite surprised to find that she remained the same size." Carroll adds: "To be sure, this is what generally happens when one eats cake; but Alice had got so much into the way of expecting nothing but out of the way things to happen, that it seemed quite dull and stupid for life to go on in the common way." Like everyone who dreams, every night, Alice walks on the surface of a globe too large to allow her to discover that the journey through language and space may be the same journey. No matter which direction she takes, all exits from the "hall of locked doors" lead into the edenic garden of paradox, the key to which is language itself. Yet Alice can comfort herself with the thought that if the cake makes her larger she can reach the key she forgot on the table before shrinking to her present size, and if she grows smaller she could creep under the door—"So either way," she concludes, "I'll get into the garden, and I don't care which happens!"

For Carroll as well as for Alice, the garden is paradise because it does not exist in space and time, but only in the uncharted space of his fairy tale, "Once upon a time . . ." And for the rest of his audience, the tales mitigate the paradox of existence in a linear narrative in which like the Knave of Hearts, we are all condemned to death, *ab ovo* after all, long before the evidence has been heard.

JUDITH CREWS

Plain Superficiality

"O, that way madness lies."
—*King Lear,* act 3, scene 2

"My name *is Alice, but—"*
"It's a stupid name enough!" Humpty Dumpty interrupted impatiently.
"What does it mean?"
—LEWIS CARROLL, *Through the Looking-Glass*

According to the rules of Carrollian logic, given any name a player may go anywhere he likes with it. He cannot, however, do anything he wants with it: the uses and misuses of names are limited by rules which apply within the system of Lewis Carroll's writings. The purpose (or porpoise, to be more in keeping with the Mock Turtle, chap. 10, *Alice's Adventures in Wonderland:*

> "No wise fish would go anywhere without a porpoise." (. . .)
> "Don't you mean 'purpose'?" said Alice.
> "I mean what I say," the Mock Turtle replied in an offended tone.

Hence this paper, headed with Super-Fish-iality, must not go anywhere without a porpoise) of this paper is to discover the limits of the game of names (= game of words, or play on words; these equivalencies will be explained under Rule 1, below) and to see how they can be applied in Carroll's writings.

One discovers, upon looking into lesser-known and seldom-quoted treatises, pamphlets, and essays by Carroll, a curious series of statements, rules, definitions, and postulates which may be used as one sees fit, or as one sees fits— thus they may be used on the Eight Fits of *The Hunting of the Snark.* They also fit the *Alice* books, unlike the words of the anonymous poem found at the end of *Alice's Adventures* (see chap. 12, "Alice's Evidence"), which do not fit the

From *enclitic* 3, no. 2 (Fall 1979). © 1979 by *enclitic.*

Queen of Hearts, according to the King of Hearts' unappreciated pun. This fits
the Cheshire Cat's claim that everyone in Wonderland is mad (i.e., in fits). The
first use of these rules is to demonstrate that "name" is the same as "word," and a
corollary is that "to name" = "to mean." These equivalencies will be shown to
be in keeping with Carroll's fictions—maybe even his nonfictions as well. (It is
true that "name" is an anagram for "mean," which anyone could have figured
out; but the true enlightenment is to derive one word from the other according
to the rules of Carroll's game.) To take the rules in order, then—

Rule 1: Words of the same length are always equal.

The arguments in support of this rule are found in one of Carroll's published word games from 1880, entitled "Doublets." Here, in reduced form, is
the gist of this word game:

> The rules of the Puzzle are simple enough. Two words are proposed,
> of the same length; and the Puzzle consists in linking these together
> by interposing other words, each of which shall differ from the next
> word *in one letter only*. That is to say, one letter may be changed in
> one of the given words, then one letter in the word so obtained, and
> so on, till we arrive at the other given word. The letters must not be
> interchanged among themselves, but each must keep to its own
> place. As an example, the word "head" may be changed into "tail"
> by interposing the words "heal, teal, tell, tall." I call the two given
> words "a Doublet," the interposed words "Links," and the entire
> series "a Chain," of which I here append an example:—
>
> HEAD
> h e a l
> t e a l
> t e l l
> t a l l
> T A I L
>
> It is, perhaps, needless to state that it is *de rigueur* that the links
> should be English words, such as might be used in good society
>
> The easiest "Doublets" are those in which the consonants in
> one word answer to consonants in the other, and the vowels to
> vowels; "head" and "tail" constitute a Doublet of this kind. Where
> this is not the case, as in "head" and "hare," the first thing to be
> done is to transform one member of the Doublet into a word whose

consonants and vowels shall answer to those in the other member (*e.g.*, "head, herd, here,") after which there is seldom much difficulty in completing the "Chain."

I am told that there is an American game involving a similar principle. I have never seen it, and can only say of its inventors, "*pereant qui ante nos nostra dixerunt!*"

"LEWIS CARROLL."

RULES

1. The words given to be linked together constitute a "Doublet," the interposed words are the "Links," and the entire series a "Chain." The object is to complete the Chain with the least possible number of Links.

2. Each word in the Chain must be formed from the preceding word by changing one letter in it, and only one. The substituted letter must occupy the same place, in the word so formed, which the discarded letter occupied in the preceding word, and all the other letters must retain their places.

3. When three or more words are given to be made into a Chain, the first and last constitute a "Doublet." The others are called "Set Links," and must be introduced into the Chain in the order in which they are given. A Chain of this kind must not contain any word twice over.

4. No word is admissible as a Link unless it (or, if it be an inflection, a word from which it comes) is to be found in the following Glossary. Comparatives and superlatives of adjectives and adverbs, when regularly formed, are regarded as "inflections" of the positive form, and are not given separately, *e.g.*, the word "new" being given, it is to be understood that "newer" and "newest" are also admissible. But nouns formed from verbs (as "reader" from "read") are *not* so regarded, and may not be used as Links unless they are to be found in the Glossary.

The Doublet WORD-NAME is thus linked as follows:

WORD
ward
*card
*care
came
NAME

*Refer to Alice's comments in chap. 8 of *Adventures*: "Why, they're only a pack of cards, after all." This is repeated in chap. 12: "Who cares for you? You're nothing but a pack of cards!"

A few explanatory comments are in order: the Glossary mentioned is not included, only the "Preface to Glossary," which along with a series of worked-out Doublets may be found in the Bibliographical material at the end of this paper. The word "doublet" itself is interesing; among its several meanings is a linguistic one, as follows: "One of two words derived from the same source by different routes of transmission." Thus we could say that the source for "word" and "name" is, in this instance, "card," and an upward route produces "word" while a downward one results in "name." Finally, "doublet" also brings to mind the word "double," which is sometimes what one sees in a looking-glass. So the linked words of a Doublet are related to mirror-images as well.

The Doublet NAME-MEAN provides a longer chain, as follows:

NAME

same

sane

sand

send

mend

mead

MEAN

Having thus united and equalled the words which we set out to join, we may continue by demonstrating how, in *Through the Looking-Glass*, ALICE can be put through GLASS:

ALICE

slice

slide

glide

glade

glads

GLASS

In this series we notice "slice," which is what Alice could not seem to do with the Looking-Glass plum-cake; "slide," which refers to what is written in the White King's Memorandum book: "The White Knight is sliding down the poker. He balances very badly," in chapter 1; "glide," which means "to float," which is what Alice does to go down the staircase in Looking-Glass House; "glade," an open space in a forest, which of course refers to the open space in Alice's memory when she forgets her name in the Wood of Forgetfulness; and "glads," an informal plural for "gladiolus," a flower, like the Talking Flowers in the garden.

After these encouraging results, we continue by showing "Where the BAKER had met with the SNARK." The process is quite a bit longer this time:

> BAKER
> bakes
> bares
> bores
> cores
> corns
> coins
> chins
> shins
> shine
> shire
> share
> shark
> SNARK

The change in the words from BAKER to SNARK (notice that there is change in the middle of the series in "coins") merely repeats in another form the last stanza of fit 8 of *The Hunting of the Snark*:

> In the midst of the word he was trying to say
> In the midst of his laughter and glee
> He had softly, and suddenly vanished away—
> For the Snark was a Boojum, you see.

The first change in the BAKER is the letter *s*, as in *softly* and *suddenly*; this *s* is repeated eight times (commemorating the eight Fits) at the ends of the words, until it is doubled in "shins," when the *s* takes its place at the head of the word, ending up in SNARK. The transformation of *B* into *S* by way of *C* also reflects that "the *S*nark was a *B*oojum, you *c*." As regards the word "shins," the locus of the double *s*, Carroll discusses what not to do with them in an article entitled "Hints For Etiquette; Or, Dining Out Made Easy":

> As a general rule, do not kick the shins of the opposite gentleman under the table, if personally unacquainted with him; your pleasantry is liable to be misunderstood—a circumstance at all times unpleasant.

Rule 2: Words of unequal length may sometimes be equal.

This rule is developed in a second of Carroll's word games, published in 1893 and called "Syzygies." In this game, the link between words consists of one or more letters in common, which yoke together the words. The following definitions and examples explain what the syzygy process is:

CHAPTER I.

SYZYGIES.

A WORD-PUZZLE.

"Phoebus, what a name!"

I. DEFINITIONS.

Def. I.

WHEN two words contain the same set of one or more consecutive letters, a copy of it, placed in a parenthesis between the two words, is called a "Syzygy," and is said to "yoke" one set to the other, and also to "yoke" each letter of one set to the corresponding letter of the other set.

Examples of Def. I.

(1)	(2)	(3)	(4)
walrus	walrus	walrus	mine
(a)	(l)	(wal)	(mi)
swallow	swallow	swallow	mimic

N.B. — In Ex. (2), the Syzygy may be regarded as yoking the "l" in "walrus" to whichever "l" in "swallow" the writer may prefer. And in Ex. (4) the Syzygy may be regarded as yoking the "mi" in "mine" to whichever "mi" in "mimic" the writer may prefer.

Def. 2.

A set of four or more words, with a Syzygy between every two, is called a "Chain," of which all but the end-words are called "Links."

Def. 3.

In a "Syzygy-Problem," two words are given, which are to form the end-words of a Chain.

Example to Def. 3.

If the given words are "walrus" and "carpenter" (the Problem might be stated in the form *"Introduce* Walrus *to* Carpenter"), the following Chain would be a solution of the Problem: —

WALRUS
(rus)
peruse
(per)
harper
(arpe)
CARPENTER.

Def. 4.

Every letter in a Chain, which is not yoked to some other, is called "waste"; but, if either of the end-words contains more than 7 letters, the extra ones are not counted as waste.

Thus, in the above Chain, the "wal" in "walrus," the "e" in "peruse," the "h" in "harper," and the "c" and the "nter" in "carpenter" are "waste": so that this Chain has 10 waste letters; but since 2 of the 5 waste letters in "carpenter" are not counted as waste, the Chain is reckoned as having only 8 waste letters.

Def. 5.

When two words contain the same letter, but these two letters are forbidden to be yoked together, these two letters are said to be "barred" with regard to each other.

A corollary demonstration of this kind of equality is provided in Carroll's "Curiosa Mathematica," part 3 of which was not published by him during his lifetime, and which contains the following interesting theorem (see page 90):

Let A B C D be a Square. Bisect A B at E, and through E draw E F at right angles to A B, and cutting D C at F. Then D F = F C.

From C draw C G = C B. Join A G, and bisect it at H. and from H draw H K at right angles to A G.

Since A B, A G are not parallel, E F, H K are not parallel. Therefore they will meet, if produced. Produce E F, and let them meet at K. Join K D, K A, K G, and K C.

THEOREM II.

AN OBTUSE ANGLE IS SOMETIMES EQUAL TO A RIGHT ANGLE

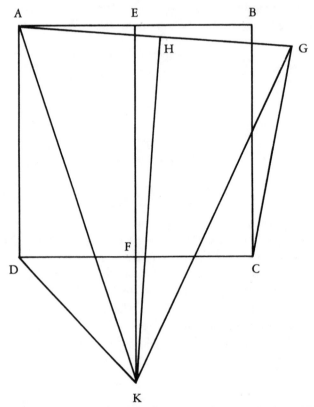

The Triangles K A H, K G H are equal, because A H = H G, H K is common, and the angles at H are right. Therefore K A = K G.

The Triangles K D F, K C F are equal, because D F = F C, F K is common, and the angles at F are right. Therefore K D = K C, and angle K D C = angle K C D.

Also D A = C B = C G.

Hence the Triangles K D A, K C G have all their sides equal. Therefore the angles K D A, K C G are equal. From these equals take the equal angles K D C, K C D. Therefore the remainders are equal: *i.e.*, the angle G C D = the angle A D C. But G C D is an obtuse angle, and A D C is a right angle.

Therefore an obtuse angle is sometimes = a right angle.

Q. E. D.

This rule will be used later on to account for numerous transformations of names in the *Alice* books and the *Snark* epic.

Rule 3: The root of any name can always be extracted.

The Carrollian example of the extraction of a name's root is to be found in an 1872 pamphlet, "The New Belfry of Christ Church, Oxford," in which the following root is given:

I. ON THE ETYMOLOGICAL SIGNIFICANCE OF
THE NEW BELFRY, CH. CH.

THE word, "Belfry" is derived from the French *bel*, "beautiful, becoming, meet," and from the German *frei*, "free, unfettered, secure, safe." Thus the word is strictly equivalent to "meatsafe," to which the new Belfry bears a resemblance so perfect as almost to amount to coincidence.

A number of etymological operations are thus justifiable in Carroll's writings according to this rule, as will be seen.

Rule 4: Once a name is inside speech acts, it can go anywhere.

Axiom: Since "speechacts" contains the same number of letters as "literature," the two are equal by Rule 1.

The details of this rule are to be found in an 1865 piece entitled "The Dynamics of a Parti-cle." Carroll's argument here consists of defining a certain number of general considerations bearing upon what must be acknowledged as the original speech act theory. That Carroll's definitions are applicable outside the realm of politics is easily seen once everything applying to politics within the article is simply ignored.

Lifting out what is thus appropriate for the game at hand, we have the following definitions, postulates, and propositions:

PLAIN SUPERFICIALITY is the character of a speech, in which any two points being taken, the speaker is found to lie wholly with regard to those two points.

PLAIN ANGER is the inclination of two voters to one another, who meet together, but whose views are not in the same direction.

Let it be granted, that a speaker may digress from any one point to any other point.

That a finite argument (i.e., one finished and disposed of), may be produced to any extent in subsequent debates.

That a controversy may be raised about any question, and at any distance from that question.

A SURD is a radical whose meaning cannot be exactly ascertained. This class comprises a very large number of particles.

The end (i.e., "the product of the extremes") justifies (i.e., "is equal to" — see Latin "aequus") the means.

If the first three Rules explain How to Do Things With Names, these Dynamics help to explain why certain transformations can take place as they do in the *Alice* books, as well as in *The Hunting of the Snark*. In particular, a system of getting from one name to the next is laid out which allows for changing, forgetting, falsifying, and replacing names, as well as for using them for various purposes.

We shall begin with falsifying names. The most spectacular example of falsifying a name is, of course, what Charles Lutwidge Dodgson did to his name in writing his fictions: it became Lewis Carroll. He published his books, then, under a pseudonym — a false name. But is it a *false* name — that is, one that is incorrect? It is surely not the proper name of the person in question — the one he would be in the habit of answering to, for one thing. According to the dictionary definition, a pseudonym is a fictitious name: i.e., a name for writing fictions. The pseudonym is the name which gives the right to write a fiction, and given the pseudo-name, one can go anywhere one likes with it to have the fiction printed, which is what Dodgson / Carroll had to do with the first and second editions of *Alice's Adventures in Wonderland*. Roger Lancelyn Green, in his book *Lewis Carroll*, has the details:

> Not only did Dodgson pay for the illustrations to his books, but he paid also to have them printed, merely employing Messrs. Macmillan & Co. to publish them on a commission basis. The work was done by the Clarendon Press at Oxford; the complete book in galley proofs was sent to Macmillan's on December 16, 1864; Tenniel checked his last proofs by the middle of June; the Press printed off two thousand copies and forty-eight were bound up early in July, most if not all of which Dodgson sent out as presents to his friends . . .
>
> Before the book was properly out, however, Tenniel wrote that he was "entirely dissatisfied with the printing of the pictures," and Dodgson — always scrupulously careful to give only the best — withdrew it from circulation . . .
>
> Meanwhile, Dodgson had the book reprinted by Messrs. Clay of London, and it was published by Macmillan's early in December,

1865, though it was dated 1866; Dodgson received the first copy on November 9, and Tenniel gave his "approval" later in the month.

This was the Second Edition, of which two thousand copies were printed.

Now, let us see how the rules function with respect to pseudonyms. Let us state that:

A pseudonym = a name (by Syzygy)

Then: pseudonyms = names for writing fictions

And, by the application of Rules 1 & 2: pseudonyms = means for righting fictions

Now, the term *means* goes in two directions, one leading to *meaning*, and the other, by the last postualte of Rule 4, to the *end*. Let us look at this postulate again:

The end justifies (i.e., "is equal to") the means.

Hence: end = means

So means = end

And: The means (names) justifies the end.

Now, justifies = gives the right to

or: = gives the write to

So: the means write the end, ergo, the name (pseudonym) writes "The End."

We have thus demonstrated how a pseudonym is a justifiable means for writing and ending fictions, according to Carroll's logic.

In a sense, all the names given within the fictions of Carroll are thus pseudonyms, because they are all fictitious names. Two good examples of writing under fictitious names or means occur in the *Alice* books. In the first case, during the trial of the Knave of Hearts' case in the *Adventures*, Alice takes away the Lizard's pencil, causing it to write with other means:

> One of the jurors had a pencil that squeaked. This, of course, Alice could *not* stand, and she went round the court and got behind him, and very soon found an opportunity of taking it away. She did it so quickly that the poor little juror (it was Bill, the Lizard) could not make out at all what had become of it; so, after hunting all about for it, he was obliged to write with one finger for the rest of the day; and this was of very little use, as it left no mark on the slate.

What the Lizard writes down "left no mark": left is the opposite of right, so the Lizard, under pseudo-means, is doing the opposite of writing.

The other incident occurs in *Through the Looking-Glass*, when Alice uses the White King's pencil to write for him:

> Alice looked on with great interest as the King took an enormous memorandum-book out of his pocket, and began writing. A sudden thought struck her, and she took hold of the end of the pencil, which came some way over his shoulder, and began writing for him.
>
> The poor King looked puzzled and unhappy, and struggled with the pencil for some time without saying anything; but Alice was too strong for him, and at last he panted out "My dear! I really *must* get a thinner pencil. I can't manage this one a bit: it writes all manner of things that I don't intend—"
>
> "What manner of things?" said the Queen, looking over the book (in which Alice had put 'The White Knight is sliding down the poker. He balances very badly') "That's not a memorandum of your feelings!"

This example proves that writers do not always intend what they write.

The best example of a pseudonym within the books is that of the Mock Turtle: he says that he used to be a real Turtle. Now his name means that he is a false turtle; if it is false, then it lies. Notice that his companion, the Gryphon, has also just been caught in an act of falsehood:

> They very soon came upon a Gryphon, lying fast asleep in the sun.

The Mock Turtle is not the only Turtle in the story with a pseudonym: he explains that the master of his school—an old Turtle—was called Tortoise by the students:

> "Why did you call him Tortoise, if he wasn't one?" Alice asked.
> "We called him Tortoise because he taught us," said the Mock Turtle angrily. "Really you are very dull!"

For the word "angrily" we could substitute "madly," and we thus have a demonstration for the expression, "O, that way madness lies." The Mock Turtle madly explains how they gave false names. We also see how, once again, the ends—in this case, teaching—justifies the name.

Madness always lies in one direction for Alice, and there are two instances which prove this axiom. The Cheshire Cat tells her that

> "In *that* direction," the Cat said, waving its right paw round, "lives a Hatter: and in *that* direction," waving the other paw, "lives a March Hare. Visit either you like: they're both mad."

She decides to visit the March Hare, then changes her mind and wishes she'd gone to visit the Hatter; it turns out that it doesn't make any difference, because she finds the two together. This is not surprising, given Rule 4 and the premise that "any two points being taken, the speaker is found to lie wholly with regard to those two points." Substituting "Cheshire Cat" for "speaker," we see that the Cat lied because the Hare and the Hatter did *not* lie in separate places; substituting "madness" for "speaker," it is evident that the Cat did not lie because madness lay wholly with regard to the two points defined by the extremities of the Hare and the Hatter. This statement may seem contradictory, until we include the further premise that "madness may digress from any one point to any other point": hence, the Hare and the Hatter may move around as they please and it will not change where madness lies. Hence, no matter which direction Alice takes, she will find that madness lies. This incident is repeated, in a transformed version, in *Through the Looking-Glass*, when Alice is walking down a road which, every time it divides, has two sign-posts pointing in the same direction, one saying "TO TWEEDLEDUM'S HOUSE" and the other "TO THE HOUSE OF TWEEDLEDEE." Madness indeed lies at this house, for after she arrives, Alice is witness to a scene of intense rage, as Tweedledum flies into a fit of fury over a rattle which Tweedledee has spoiled.

The changing of names is another observable phenomenon in the books: we have already seen the transformation of BAKER to SNARK. We can also observe that the Mad Hatter and the March Hare of the *Adventures* become Hatta and Haigha of *Looking-Gasss*; that Alice is turned from a Pawn into a Queen, as well as to a Fabulous Monster, according to the Unicorn. The Red Queen, at the end of *Through the Looking-Glass*, is transformed into the Black Kitten: this transformation is really a trans-ferral, because the Queen, who has no fur, ends up as a kitten with fur. The kitten is thus a re-fur-ance point in the books.

A subclass of transformations is illustrated by the use of pronouns in the books. Pronouns, in their function as replacements for nouns, are clearly related to SURDS, those radicals with unascertained meanings. We see that, in some cases, pronouns are names, and in others they are means. The latter case is exemplified by the exchange between the Duck and the Mouse in the *Adventures*:

> "and even Stigand, the patriotic archbishop of Canterbury, found it advisable—"
>
> "Found *what*?" said the Duck.
>
> "Found *it*," the Mouse replied rather crossly: "of course you know what 'it' means."
>
> "I know what 'it' means well enough, when I find a thing," said the Duck: "it's generally a frog or a worm. The question is, what did the archbishop find?"

We have here a SURD par excellence, since the meaning of "it" cannot be ascertained. The Duck's question also demonstrates a controversy being raised about a point, and at any distance from that point, since it is unquestionable that "frogs" or "worms" would be at a great distance from what the archbishop found.

Pronouns as names appear with Nobody and Somebody, who show up (or do not show up, as the case may be) in both the *Alice* books. At the Knave's trial, a letter (or rather, "a set of verses") is produced by the White Rabbit:

> "I haven't opened it yet," said the White Rabbit; "but it seems to be a letter, written by the prisoner to — to somebody."
>
> "It must have been that," said the King, "unless it was written to nobody, which isn't usual, you know."

This letter is a focal point of interest with regard to names, since the main question concerns who wrote it. The Knave of Hearts denies authorship, claiming that "there's no name signed at the end." If there is "no name" *signed* at the end, then there *is* a signature. The King replies:

> "If you didn't sign it," said the King, "that only makes the matter worse. You *must* have meant some mischief, or else you'd have signed your name like an honest man."

This explains why the Knave of Hearts is on trial: he is being brought to justice, or rather, being justified, for not having signed his name. We know that the end justifies the means, meaning that the end of justice will be a sentence. The anonymous sentences to which the Knave claims no rights (writes), are the means by which no name is sentenced. The Queen sentences everyone by shouting "Off with his head," which is capital punishment, turning capital letters into small letters. The letter in question is seen to turn into verses.

Nobody shows up again in *Through the Looking-Glass*, when the King asks Alice to look down the road and see who is coming:

> "Just look along the road, and tell me if you can see either of them."
>
> "I see nobody on the road," said Alice.
>
> "I only wish *I* had such eyes," the King remarked in a fretful tone. "To be able to see Nobody! And at that distance too!"

When Alice at last sees Somebody, it turns out to be the Anglo-Saxon messenger, who, when asked by the King "Who did you pass on the road?" replies, as might be expected, "Nobody."

The Anglo-Saxon Messenger brings up at this point the proper use of English in Carroll's writings. In the *Adventures* we find the following:

"In that case," said the Dodo solemnly, rising to its feet, "I move that the meeting adjourn, for the immediate adoption of more energetic remedies—"

"Speak English!" said the Eaglet. "I don't know the meaning of half those long words, and, what's more, I don't believe you do either!"

The Eaglet is quite correct in demanding that the Dodo speak English, for the Dodo's sentence contains six words which do not have their etymological origins in Anglo-Saxon but rather in Latin or in Greek. Let us observe the roots of these words:

move: Middle English moven, from Norman French mover, variant of Old French moveir, from Latin movere, to move.

adjourn: Middle English adjournen, from Old French ajourner, "to put off to an appointed day": a-, to, from Latin ad- jour, day, from Late Latin diurnum, day, from diurnus, daily, from dies, day.

immediate: Late Latin immediatus: Latin in-, not mediatus, past participle of mediare, to be in the middle.

energetic: Late Latin energia, from Greek energeia, coined by Aristotle from energes, energos, active, at work: en-, at ergon, work.

remedies: Middle English remedie, from Norman French, from Latin remedium, medicine: re-, again mederi, to heal.

adoption: Latin adoptare, to choose for oneself: ad-, to optare, to choose, desire.

It is not coincidental then that the Eaglet's irritation interrupts the Dodo's speech. All the birds are irritated because they are wet and the Mouse's speech about William the Conqueror has not dried them off. Recall also that the Mouse began his story with the words "William the Conqueror" and ended it with the word "Norman": these associations bring up the painful reminder to all Englishmen that the Norman-French language invasion brought in by William the Conqueror in 1066 put a brutal end to the *true* English language, corrupting an otherwise pure Anglo-Saxon with Latin and Greek. (We can now comprehend the Anglo-Saxon attitudes of Haigha in *Through the Looking-Glass*.) The Anglo-Saxon names, in other words, lost their means. Observe, then, that the first and last words of the Dodo's sentence are the two Norman-French words in the list, namely "move" and "remedies," and the Eaglet's reaction is entirely in order. The Dodo tries to repair the damage by re-sentencing, using this time no latinate words:

> "What I was going to say," said the Dodo in an offended tone, "was,
> that the best thing to get us dry would be a Caucus-race."

Sure enough, every single word from "that" to "race" is pure English, even though two of the words ("get" and "race") have their ultimate roots in Old Norse: but the Old English and the Old Norse got along, so to speak, anyway.

that: Middle English that, Old English thaet
the: Middle English the, Old English the
best: Middle English best, Old English bet(e)st
thing: Middle English thing, Old English thing
to: Middle English to, Old English to, te
get: Middle English getten, gat, getten, from Old Norse geta, gat,
    getinn
us: Middle English us, Old English us
dry: Middle English dry, drye, Ole English dryge
would, will: Middle English willen, wolde, woldest, Old English
    wyllan, wolde, woldest
be: Middle English be(e)n, be(o)n, Old English beon
a: Middle English a(n), Old English an, an, one
Caucus: Virginia Algonquin word for "counselor" recorded by
    Captain John Smith—a white, Anglo-Saxon Protestant
race: Middle English ra(a)s, Old Norse ras.

(N.B.: all these etymologies have been taken verbatim—well, almost verbatim—from *The American Heritage Dictionary of the English Language*, ed. William Morris (Boston: Houghton Mifflin Co., 1969); it is not known where they came from before that.)

Not speaking English, then, causes many misunderstandings. In *The Hunting of the Snark*, the Baker exclaims:

> "I said it in Hebrew—I said it in Dutch—
> I said it in German and Greek:
> But I wholly forgot (and it vexes me much)
> That English is what you speak!"
>
>   (fit 4, st. 5)

The "it" to which he refers is here the fact that the Baker has been forewarned that "if ever I meet with a Boojum, that day, / In a moment (of this I am sure), / I shall softly and suddenly vanish away—" (fit 3, last stanza). The Baker has told the crew of the ship about the danger he is in, but he did it in a language which no one understood. His reason is that he has forgotten, not the

English language itself, but the fact that English is what the crew speaks. Now it is precisely this same Baker who has forgotten his own name on boarding the ship, and the result of this lapse of memory is that he will answer to anything:

> He would answer to "Hi!" or to any loud cry,
> Such as "Fry me!" or "Fritter my wig!"
> To "What-you-may-call-um!" or "What-was-his-name!"
> But especially "Thing-um-a-jig!"
>
> (fit 1, st. 9)

Alice, too, answers to a name which is not "Alice" when the White Rabbit mistakes her for Mary Ann, apparently his maid. She also decides, when she is not sure of her identity after having fallen down the rabbit-hole, that she will not come out until "they" call her by the right name:

> "It'll be no use their putting their heads down and saying, 'Come up again, dear!' I shall only look up and say, 'Who am I, then? Tell me that first, and then, if I like being that person, I'll come up: if not, I'll stay down here till I'm somebody else' — "

Alice will wait until she's called the right name, for the wrong one will mean that she will become a person she dislikes, such as Ada or Mabel. Naming thus means calling something correctly, or identifying it so that it can be found again. Alice only loses her name once, in the Woods with the Fawn, but she finds it again; this is much better than the clock which is only right twice a day, discussed by Carroll in "The Two Clocks." His argument is as follows:

> Which is better, a clock that is right only once a year, or a clock that is right twice every day? "The latter," you reply, "unquestionably." Very good, now attend.
> I have two clocks: one doesn't go at all, and the other loses a minute a day: which would you prefer? "The losing one," you answer, "without a doubt." Now observe: the one which loses a minute a day has to lose twelve hours, or seven hundred and twenty minutes before it is right again, consequently it is only right once in two years, whereas the other is evidently right as often as the time it points to comes round, which happens twice a day.
> So you've contradicted yourself *once*.
> "Ah, but," you say, "what's the use of its being right twice a day, if I can't tell when the time comes?"

Why, suppose the clock points to eight o'clock, don't you see that the clock is right *at* eight o'clock? Consequently, when eight o'clock comes round your clock is right.

"Yes, I see *that*," you reply.

Very good, then you've contradicted yourself *twice*: now get out of the difficulty as best you can, and don't contradict yourself again if you can help it.

You *might* go on to ask, "How am I to know when eight o'clock *does* come? My clock will not tell me." Be patient: very good; then your rule is this: keep your eye fixed on your clock, and *the moment it is right* it will be eight o'clock. "But —," you say, There, that'll do; the more you argue the farther you get from the point, so it will be as well to stop.

The problem is that the name of the hour as told by the clock does no good in telling the time: it is about as useful as Alice's trying to decide if she really is Alice by reciting from memory what she used to know: when she cannot recite her lessons properly, she decides that her name must be different. Notice also in the above article that a PLAIN ANGER is about to arise, because the views of the two speakers are not in the same direction — this is the same thing as Plain Madness.

The ultimate name-change would not be, in Carroll's terms, simply a different word: the entire code would be changed in the best transformations. And so indeed we find that Carroll left behind an "Alphabet Cipher" for the changing of any letter in the alphabet into any other. This is the supreme application of Plain Superficiality: "the character of a letter (by Doublet), in which any two points being taken, the letters are found to lie wholly with regard to those two points." Here is the cipher and the instructions for its use (see page 101):

EXPLANATION

EACH column of this table forms a dictionary of symbols representing the alphabet: thus, in the A column, the symbol is the same as the letter represented; in the B column, A is represented by B, B by C, and so on.

To use the table, some word or sentence should be agreed on by two correspondents. This may be called the "key-word," or "key-sentence," and should be carried in the memory only.

In sending a message, write the key-word over it, letter for letter, repeating it as often as may be necessary: the letters of the key-word will indicate which column is to be used in translating each letter of

THE ALPHABET-CIPHER

	A	B	C	D	E	F	G	H	I	J	K	L	M	N	O	P	Q	R	S	T	U	V	W	X	Y	Z	
A	a	b	c	d	e	f	g	h	i	j	k	l	m	n	o	p	q	r	s	t	u	v	w	x	y	z	A
B	b	c	d	e	f	g	h	i	j	k	l	m	n	o	p	q	r	s	t	u	v	w	x	y	z	a	B
C	c	d	e	f	g	h	i	j	k	l	m	n	o	p	q	r	s	t	u	v	w	x	y	z	a	b	C
D	d	e	f	g	h	i	j	k	l	m	n	o	p	q	r	s	t	u	v	w	x	y	z	a	b	c	D
E	e	f	g	h	i	j	k	l	m	n	o	p	q	r	s	t	u	v	w	x	y	z	a	b	c	d	E
F	f	g	h	i	j	k	l	m	n	o	p	q	r	s	t	u	v	w	x	y	z	a	b	c	d	e	F
G	g	h	i	j	k	l	m	n	o	p	q	r	s	t	u	v	w	x	y	z	a	b	c	d	e	f	G
H	h	i	j	k	l	m	n	o	p	q	r	s	t	u	v	w	x	y	z	a	b	c	d	e	f	g	H
I	i	j	k	l	m	n	o	p	q	r	s	t	u	v	w	x	y	z	a	b	c	d	e	f	g	h	I
J	j	k	l	m	n	o	p	q	r	s	t	u	v	w	x	y	z	a	b	c	d	e	f	g	h	i	J
K	k	l	m	n	o	p	q	r	s	t	u	v	w	x	y	z	a	b	c	d	e	f	g	h	i	j	K
L	l	m	n	o	p	q	r	s	t	u	v	w	x	y	z	a	b	c	d	e	f	g	h	i	j	k	L
M	m	n	o	p	q	r	s	t	u	v	w	x	y	z	a	b	c	d	e	f	g	h	i	j	k	l	M
N	n	o	p	q	r	s	t	u	v	w	x	y	z	a	b	c	d	e	f	g	h	i	j	k	l	m	N
O	o	p	q	r	s	t	u	v	w	x	y	z	a	b	c	d	e	f	g	h	i	j	k	l	m	n	O
P	p	q	r	s	t	u	v	w	x	y	z	a	b	c	d	e	f	g	h	i	j	k	l	m	n	o	P
Q	q	r	s	t	u	v	w	x	y	z	a	b	c	d	e	f	g	h	i	j	k	l	m	n	o	p	Q
R	r	s	t	u	v	w	x	y	z	a	b	c	d	e	f	g	h	i	j	k	l	m	n	o	p	q	R
S	s	t	u	v	w	x	y	z	a	b	c	d	e	f	g	h	i	j	k	l	m	n	o	p	q	r	S
T	t	u	v	w	x	y	z	a	b	c	d	e	f	g	h	i	j	k	l	m	n	o	p	q	r	s	T
U	u	v	w	x	y	z	a	b	c	d	e	f	g	h	i	j	k	l	m	n	o	p	q	r	s	t	U
V	v	w	x	y	z	a	b	c	d	e	f	g	h	i	j	k	l	m	n	o	p	q	r	s	t	u	V
W	w	x	y	z	a	b	c	d	e	f	g	h	i	j	k	l	m	n	o	p	q	r	s	t	u	v	W
X	x	y	z	a	b	c	d	e	f	g	h	i	j	k	l	m	n	o	p	q	r	s	t	u	v	w	X
Y	y	z	a	b	c	d	e	f	g	h	i	j	k	l	m	n	o	p	q	r	s	t	u	v	w	x	Y
Z	z	a	b	c	d	e	f	g	h	i	j	k	l	m	n	o	p	q	r	s	t	u	v	w	x	y	Z
	A	B	C	D	E	F	G	H	I	J	K	L	M	N	O	P	Q	R	S	T	U	V	W	X	Y	Z	

the message, the symbols for which should be written underneath: then copy out the symbols only, and destroy the first paper. It will now be impossible for any one, ignorant of the key-word, to decipher the message, even with the help of the table.

For example, let the key-word be *vigilance*, and the message "meet me on Tuesday evening at seven," the first paper will read as follows—

v i g i l a n c e v i g i l a n c e v i g i l a n c e v i
m e e t m e o n t u e s d a y e v e n i n g a t s e v e n
h m k b x e b p x p m y l l y r x i i q t o l t f g z z v

The second will contain only "h m k b x e b p x p m y l l y r x i i q t o l t f g z z v."

The receiver of the message can, by the same process, retranslate it into English.

N.B. If this table be lost, it can easily be written out from memory, by observing that the first symbol in each column is the same as the letter naming the column, and that they are continued downwards in alphabetical order. Of course it would only be necessary to write out the particular columns required by the key-word: such a paper, however, should not be preserved, as it would afford means for discovering the key-word.

The final rule will have to be that any letter is equal to any other letter, given the proper key word.

The end of this paper should justify the means, i.e., the name. So, if the name of this paper is called "Plain Superficiality," then, to paraphrase the White Knight, the name of the paper really is "The Name of the Paper"; the paper is called "The Justification of the Ways and Means"; and the paper itself really *is* about to end, with the words of the White Knight, curiously applicable here:

> "It's long," said the Knight, "but it's very, *very* beautiful. Everybody that hears me sing it — either it brings the *tears* into their eyes, or else —"
>
> "Or else what?" said Alice, for the Knight had made a sudden pause.
>
> "Or else it doesn't, you know."

EDWARD GUILIANO

Lewis Carroll,
Laughter and Despair,
and The Hunting of the Snark

*T*he Hunting of the Snark (1876), Lewis Carroll's third and final literary masterpiece, has rested for more than a hundred years in the shadow of *Alice in Wonderland* (1865) and *Through the Looking-Glass* (1871). It is a poem with much of the *Alices* in it, "a kind of *Alice in Wonderland* without Alice," as one commentator has remarked; "it extends and illuminates some of the themes and practices of the two Alice books." Dreams, death, probings into the nature of being, reminders of the inescapability of time, and a quest motif figure in all three works. Moreover, just as one senses terror lurking beneath the surface of the *Alice* books, one senses terror and despair throughout the overtly humorous *Snark*. This tension between the comic tone and the underlying anxieties is perhaps the poem's most distinguishing and fascinating characteristic.

I

In recent years the *Snark* has become "a much more serious piece of humor than it ever was for the Victorians." Intellectuals now find its lurking terrors immediate and compelling. Living at Oxford through mid- and late-Victorian England, C. L. Dodgson's subconscious was surely infused with the anxieties of his age, and a case can be made for reading the poem's subtext as a record of some of the uncertainties that troubled intellectuals of the period, especially the horrors of confronting death and nothingness in a purposeless, post-Darwinian world. But while twentieth-century readers will readily entertain such an assertion,

From *Lewis Carroll: A Celebration: Essays on the Occasion of the 150th Anniversary of the Birth of Charles Lutwidge Dodgson.* © 1982 by Edward Guiliano. Clarkson N. Potter, 1982.

Dodgson and his contemporaries would have dismissed it as ludicrous. For them, *The Hunting of the Snark* was a delirious and harmless flight of imagination very much in one of the mainstreams of Victorian comedy.

The Hunting of the Snark, a heroic nonsense poem in eight episodes, is in the nonsense tradition of Thomas Hood and William Schwenck Gilbert; indeed, Dodgson may well have been influenced when writing the *Snark* by Gilbert's *Bab Ballads* (1869–73). Although *The Hunting of the Snark* is a relatively long comic poem, Victorian readers could regularly find shorter works of its kind in the comic weeklies that flourished in the 1860s and 1870s. One of the reasons the *Snark* continues to amuse adult readers is, according to Donald Gray, that it is a work of a man who "spent a good deal of time watching and practicing the habits of nineteenth-century writers whose profession it was to amuse adults." Even a cursory overview of Dodgson's life reveals how intimate he was with the comic writing and theater of his age. It is not surprising that many of the common techniques and conventions of Victorian comic writing are found in Carroll's works, and that to some extent *The Hunting of the Snark* is, as Gray suggests, an extraordinarily skillful and confident exercise in some of the means by which nineteenth-century writers entertained their contemporaries.

Seen in this context, we can understand that the *Snark*'s initial reviewers were not so much surprised or uncomfortable with the poem's genre as they were puzzled by its nonsense. The first reviews ranged from mixed to bad—frequently finding little of the whimsy and escape of the *Alices* in it. For the Victorians, at least, it seems there was no tension between the nonsense ballad and the underlying anxieties—but only failed fantasy or delirious nonsense, depending upon the reader's personal taste.

Dodgson himself was at a loss to explain the poem. He admitted this on several occasions. In 1880, for example, when one of his child-friends asked him "why don't you explain the Snark?" he replied "'*because* I *can't*.' Are you able to explain things which you don't yourself understand?" In an often quoted letter to a group of children he wrote: "As to the meaning of the *Snark*? I'm very much afraid I didn't mean anything but nonsense! Still, you know, words mean more than we mean to express when we use them; so a whole book ought to mean a great deal more than the writer meant. So, whatever good meanings are in the book, I'm very glad to accept as the meaning of the book."

We do know something about the poem's genesis. Dodgson recorded an account of a stroll he took on the Surrey Downs on July 18, 1874:

> I was walking on a hillside, alone, one bright summer day, when suddenly there came into my head one line of verse—one solitary line—"For the Snark was a Boojum, you see." I knew not what it

meant, then: I know not what it means, now; but I wrote it down: and, some time afterwards, the rest of the stanza occurred to me, that being its last line: and so by degrees, at odd moments during the next year or two, the rest of the poem pieced itself together, that being the last stanza.

Morton Cohen has placed this walk in a most revealing context. It was taken when Dodgson was deeply distressed and exhausted. The previous night he had stayed up nursing a dying cousin—his twenty-two-year-old godchild, Charles Wilcox. The walk provided Dodgson with a means of escape from the painful reality he faced at home. His flash of inspiration, his line from the world of nonsense, Cohen believes, can easily be seen as a natural, personal defense. Although there is no outright evidence that Lewis Carroll himself made any connection between the *Snark* and the tragic case of Charles Wilcox, Cohen assures us that there surely is one. The line "For the Snark *was* a Boojum, you see" flowed unquestionably from deep, unsettled springs of imagination. In this line and others in the poem we can see reflected Dodgson's deep personal dreads and anxieties.

The Victorians' attitude toward death and dying was complex and is often different than our own; yet, regardless of context, Dodgson clearly was anxious over and preoccupied with death. One can see some evidence of this even in the "Easter Greeting" he wrote to accompany the first edition of the *Snark*, where we find him electing to write about "when my turn comes to walk through the valley of shadows." Some readers will see more evidence in the understandable but somewhat surprising fact that he regarded his father's death (at age sixty-eight) "the deepest sorrow I have known in life." And before his fifty-second birthday, for a better illustration, he was calling himself an "unconventional old man" on certain points and a "confirmed old bachelor, who is now well over fifty." His concern with death is ever present in the preface to *Sylvie and Bruno* (1889), and implicit as well as explicit references to death and dying are not infrequent in his letters and diaries. William Empson was the first to point out that both of the *Alice* books "keep to the topic of death."

Although the death jokes that pervade the *Alices* do not contribute to the progress of the story, their striking frequency causes the reader to maintain a subtle awareness of the topic throughout the stories. No doubt intimations of death were never far from the consciousness of the author while he was writing; they were at least active in his subconscious. Elizabeth Sewell has pointed out that nonsense holds a fear of nothingness quite as great as its fear of everythingness. She suggests that it is perhaps simpler to think of the fear of death (which she agrees is a crucial topic of both the *Alice* books) as a fear of nothingness. Consider in the Tweedledum and Tweedledee chapter of *Through the Looking-Glass* that the twins challenge Alice with the most horrifying suggestions regarding existence and the nature of nonexistence. They tell her she is just a character in the sleeping Red King's dream, and if he were to awake, " 'you'd go out—bang!— just like a candle! . . . You know very well you're not real.' 'I *am* real!' said Alice, and began to cry." How similar going out like a candle is to softly and suddenly vanishing away at the sight of a Boojum.

This positing of existence (being) as life in a dream occurs repeatedly in the *Alice* books. Dreams figure prominently in the *Snark* as well. The Snark—or a snark—exists, being clearly defined in the Barrister's dream. A snark (another snark?) exists for the Baker—every night he engages "in a dreamy delirious fight" with it. For the Baker, at least, life and dream become fused.

Not surprisingly, Dodgson—acutely aware of death and fascinated by states of being (which include not only dying but dreaming and even spiritualism)—was also more than normally frustrated by the limits real time presents. In *Alice in Wonderland*, for example, the familiar White Rabbit, always late, always checking his watch, is Carroll's comic expression of his own, and others', anxious preoccupation with the passage of time. In 1881 Dodgson resigned his Mathematical Lectureship to have more time to devote to writing and other projects. Within a few years he had "retired from society," since he resented the time "lost" on social affairs. Still in his fifties he would write, "Friends wonder sometimes at my refusing all social invitations now, and taking no holidays. But when old age has begun, and the remaining years are *certainly* not many, and the work one wishes to do, before the end comes, is *almost* certainly more than there is time for, I think one cares less for so-called 'pass-times.' I want the time to go more *slowly*, not more *quickly!*" Here one is reminded of the Red Queen's famous dictum, "it takes all the running *you* can do, to keep in the same place." Throughout his life, in his letters and in his diary, Dodgson expresses his distress over unfulfilled expectations and about opportunities lost in the continued lapse of moments. Consider this diary entry:

> Dec: 31   (Th.). 1863   Here, at the close of another year, how much of neglect, carelessness, and sin have I to remember! I had hoped, during the year, to have made a beginning in a parochial work, to have thrown off habits of evil, to have advanced in my work at Christ Church. How little, next to nothing, has been done of all this! Now I have a fresh year before me: once more let me set myself to do something worthy of life "before I go hence, and be no more seen."

Here is Dodgson bemoaning his unfulfilled plans. The year is ended; another year has passed, a year gone forever—the time before his death is dwindling.

But the thirty-one-year-old clergyman does not call it death. His dread is apparent, and what he dreads, in his own words, is going hence and being no more seen. Being no more? Being seen no more? How, too, like a confrontation with a Boojum.

II

In the *Snark* the Bellman is a constant reminder of time. Curiously, the Bellman is a character almost totally neglected by modern critics of *The Hunting of the Snark*. For the Bellman is, after all, the central character in the poem. A figure of power and authority, he organizes the expedition and remains in charge of it and of the ship. He knows how to hunt a snark and is able to define its five qualities. Despite his questionable ability to handle the voyage, he sees the hunt through to success: They do find a snark. The Bellman is the central character also in that he is the character most often present in the narrative, and when he is present he is always in possession of his bell. In all of Henry Holiday's approved illustrations of the poem, the Bellman is shown holding the bell—often ringing, tingling it. (For an example, see the frontispiece to the *Snark*.)

The Bellman's bell is an ordinary school bell, which is struck to mark off time. *Bellman* is, of course, another term for town crier. On a ship, a bell is rung at half-hour intervals to mark off the time in a watch. The bells of a school, too, mark time. And church bells not only mark off time, they also announce death. The Bellman and his bell are both symbolic and real reminders of time—its steady passage and its inevitability. The pulsating repetitions of the bell's ringing signal to the reader the regular and perpetual movement of time. Holiday's illustrations of the Bellman even suggest a wise Father Time figure. Another interesting aspect of the approved illustrations is that all but one contain the figure of the Bellman and his bell—haunting reminders of the inescapability of time. An image of this haunting temporality occurs when the Barrister falls into a dreamful sleep in the sixth fit. It is the sound of the Bellman's bell in his ear that awakens him and cuts short his dreams. The Bellman's centrality as a character indicates the centrality of time in the poem.

Martin Gardner interprets *The Hunting of the Snark* as being:

> a poem about being and nonbeing, an existential poem, a poem of existential agony. The Bellman's map is the map that charts the course of humanity; blank because we possess no information about where we are or whither we drift. . . . The Snark is, in Paul Tillich's fashionable phrase, every man's ultimate concern. This is the great search motif of the poem, the quest for an ultimate good.

But this motif is submerged in a stronger motif, the dread, the agon-
izing dread, of ultimate failure. The Boojum is more than death. It
is the end of all searching. It is final, absolute extinction.

Naturally, the Snark can represent different things to different people; the
Barrister sees it one way, the Baker perhaps another. The ending can also be read
differently; it can be equated by some with a conventional, even Christian,
death or by others with an existential nothingness. I agree that the Boojum can
be viewed as an existential horror. It seems to be an expression of Dodgson's
dread, his nightmare, his anxiety toward facing the end of his being. The equation of the ending with absolute extinction expresses a powerful anti-Christian,
anti-Protestant belief, something Dodgson would never consciously confess. In
the pessimism of the *Alice* books, and in the horror of the *Snark*, there is no evidence for Christian hope of salvation. (The figure of Hope does appear in the
Snark as part of Henry Holiday's iconography, but not in the text—she is rendered in the illustration to the fourth fit, paradoxically carrying the ship's anchor
on this ill-fated voyage. Her image may at first function traditionally, suggesting hope and virtue, but for me she provides no affirmation of Christian values.
On the contrary, her image is ultimately an inverted image, an emblem of virtue
failed, of despair and frustration.)

In the third fit of the *Snark*, the Baker, a character sometimes viewed as
Dodgson's satirical self-portrait, expresses his dread of the Boojum. He explains
his emotional response to his uncle's warning to "Beware of the day, if your snark
be a Boojum!"

> It is this, it is this that oppresses my soul,
>   When I think of my uncle's last words:
> And my heart is like nothing so much as a bowl
>   Brimming over with quivering curds!

It is easy and justifiable to equate this reaction with a state of acute existential nausea, which Gardner suggests. The Baker also describes what can be viewed
as a state of existential dread:

> I engage with the Snark—every night after dark—
>   In a dreamy delirious fight:
> I serve it with greens in those shadowy scenes,
>   And I use it for striking a light.

This stanza provides an excellent illustration of the tension that exists between the comic tone and the underlying terror that characterizes the poem for
readers today. It also provides us with a glimpse at the nature of Carroll's artistic
temperament. The first two lines, "I engage with the Snark—every night after

dark — / In a dreamy delirious fight:" can be read as a statement that parallels Dodgson's own experience. He was an insomniac kept awake at least partially by haunting and troubling thoughts. In fact, he published a book of puzzles devised to help ease the pain of his sleeplessness — some mental work to help free his mind of its troubling thoughts, thoughts that surely occurred to many of his contemporaries as well. In the preface to that book, *Pillow Problems* (1893), he writes of the realization that: "There are skeptical thoughts, which seem for the moment to uproot the firmest faith; there are blasphemous souls; there are unholy thoughts, which torture with their hateful presence, the fancy that would fain be pure."

But although we can find suggestions of Dodgson's anxieties in the Baker's dread, in the closing lines, "I serve it with greens in those shadowy scenes, / And I use it for striking a light," we find only whimsy and nonsense. They change the tone completely.

If we view the stanza's opening lines as being somewhat autobiographical, and if we view certain critical lines, such as the paramount "The Snark *was* a Boojum, you see," as springing up as raw psychic impulses from Dodgson's troubled unconscious, then we might view much of the poem's humor as springing up in Dodgson's self-defense and its laughter as liberating, tension-relieving. These impulses would insulate and isolate the moments of despair and would prevent them from spreading — which is consistent with Bergson's and Freud's beliefs that comedy enables us to assert a degree of control (mastery) over fears, or threats, by removing them from our conscious and immediate world and setting them off at a comfortable distance.

But let us not forget that Carroll's literary works were composed as entertainments. They were his hobby, his own entertainment as much as an entertainment for others — principally his child-friends. Initially they grew from spontaneous impulses, and later they were crafted into highly wrought stories and poems. As a hobby, writing provided Dodgson with a diversion, an escape, really, from his sober and demanding duties as a mathematics don and as a clergyman, as well as from his responsibilities as the head of a large family. By discussing some of Dodgson's apparent anxieties, I do not want to suggest that he was a deeply troubled man; on the contrary, by all accounts he seems to have been in reasonably sound mental and physical health. If he was a bit eccentric and perhaps even suspect on some grounds, he appeared happy and tolerably well adjusted. I have been suggesting in fact that his "entertainments" and his humor helped him to cope with the anxieties of his own life and those of his age. When he relaxed and left his mind soar without restraint, it is not unnatural that a few deep-seated dreads were in evidence. (Need I even suggest the techniques of psychoanalysis?) It is also not surprising that when these anxieties emerged, they were accompanied by laughter; indeed, such a response is natural and healthy. At times he was able to defeat pain, to achieve escape from the troubling problems common to his age through laughter; it denied pain its province. Sometimes his humor is like that of Freud's prisoner, who remarks, on his way to the gallows: "Well, this is a good beginning to the week." It is a rebellious assertion by the ego that in the face of inevitable extinction, it is somehow invulnerable.

At other times Carroll's humor is (as I have suggested earlier) conscious and skillful craftsmanship in the Victorian comic tradition. This humor is often the reshaping of the gifts of his comic muse. Whether the humor in Carroll's writings is the result of a spontaneous or a willed activity, it can be viewed as a means for Dodgson to control his world. Humor was a means for him to order his experience. In his life and in his art Dodgson continually sought rufage, temporary escape, from life's exigencies through order and reason. This is evidenced in both his books and his personal habits. Witness his *Pillow Problems* as one example. Even witness Dodgson's playful battle with his unconscious in the preface he wrote to the *Snark*. Unable to comprehend the nonsense "Then the bowsprit got mixed with the rudder sometimes," he invents a ludicrous explanation. In doing so, he asserts control. The gaining of control through order is even evidenced in the structural integrity of his literary works—the *Snark* tightly organized in a poetic ballad form, the *Alices* each carefully written in twelve chapters—in the prosody of his poems, in the logic of his dialogues, his puns, his narratives structures. *The Hunting of the Snark* is, as Michael Holquist has justly pointed out, the most nonsensical nonsense that Carroll created, and it best exemplifies what his career and all his books sought to do: achieve pure order.

On the thin line separating laughter from despair in Lewis Carroll's writings there is an anxiety-ridden outlook that is rooted in Dodgson's life. From the child's dreamworld of *Alice in Wonderland* with its strange and comical characters—a world in which escape really seems possible—to *Through the Looking-Glass*, pessimism is readily evidenced. Escape is not possible in the later book. The fears over existence and time are bound up into a metaphor of life as a chessboard and all its people as but pawns and pieces. In this game, this book, there is a determinism, a fatalism, that taints much of the mirth and depressingly eliminates individual possibilities. *The Hunting of the Snark* can be read as a statement of despair over the state of being—Dodgson's despair over the threat of nonexistence and the inescapability of time. This poem, which on the literal level has so many humorous moments, turns out to be the saddest of Carroll's writings. The ending is not at all funny. One character vanishes, and another, the Bellman, remains a grave and depressing figure. He has, after all, but one notion of navigation, and that is to toll his bell.

DONALD RACKIN

Love and Death
in Carroll's Alices

Considering the internal and external evidence, most readers new to Lewis Carroll would naturally expect to find love playing a major role in the central narratives of his *Alices*. *Wonderland* ends (as does *Alice's Adventures under Ground*) with remarks about Alice's "simple and loving heart"; and *Through the Looking-Glass* begins with a poem declaring that Charles Dodgson's "love-gift of a fairy-tale" will elicit a "loving smile" from his dearest little reader, his beloved companion and model Alice Liddell. For Dodgson devoted a great measure of his energy in a life-long service to his love for little girls. Moreover, as a true amateur par excellence, in his everyday affairs and amusements, and throughout his letters, diaries and lesser literary works—from the satirical "Love's Railway Guide" of his juvenilia to his final maudlin opus *Sylvie and Bruno Concluded* (which ends with an angel's voice whispering "IT IS LOVE")— love was clearly one of his dominant concerns. As Dodgson wrote to an eleven-year-old correspondent when he was fifty-nine, "*love* is the best thing in all the world."

Lewis Carroll is of course Dodgson's "own invention" (if you want to see him as he sometimes imagined himself, look at the frontispiece to *Looking-Glass*), as are Alice and the White Knight. But in real life, too, Dodgson played a genuine Christian knight, giving much of himself gratuitously in authentic, loving generosity to the countless Alices, Ediths and Ethels of his wide acquaintance. Love itself was also a crucial topic in Dodgson's milieu, a world where, in fact, some despairing Oxford contemporaries had already turned to love as the only possible refuge on the "darkling plain" of their faithless age ("Dover Beach,"

From *English Language Notes* 20, no. 2 (December 1982). © 1982 by the Regents of the University of Colorado.

incidentally, was published just about halfway between *Wonderland* and *Through the Looking-Glass*).

Furthermore, the *Alice* adventures themselves offer a variety of internal evidence perhaps more convincing than these biographical and historical facts or than the books' rather sentimental frames (whose relations to the actual adventures remain somewhat problematical), evidence that would also lead readers to expect more on the subject of love from these works. After all, THE KING AND QUEEN OF HEARTS stand prominently at the center of the punning world of Wonderland, and a spirit of love is expected to inform the audience's emotional response to a child protagonist like Alice. Love also lies at the base of several of those important nursery rhymes Alice unwittingly subverts. And despite the Cheshire Cat's assertion that madness reigns in Wonderland, the Ugly Duchess declares with equal finality, " 'Tis love, 'tis love, that makes the world go round!"

But Alice herself, in much the same uncontrollable way that she twists the loving and sentimental messages of her nursery rhymes into dark visions of unloving, predatory, post-Darwinian nature, reminds the insincere Duchess of the Duchess's own earlier declaration: the world goes round, Alice suggests, "by everybody minding their own business!" Indeed, Alice's curt, unloving deflation of love here mirrors an important facet of Carroll's characteristically unsentimental wit, particularly as it works within the *Alices*. Despite the great loving care Dodgson expended in preparing the beautiful *Under Ground* manuscript as a love-gift for his dear Alice Liddell, near the manuscript's end he carefully placed his final drawing — the mad Queen of Hearts, in his own later estimate a heartless "blind and aimless Fury," as alien from love and love-gifts as any fantasy creature could conceivably be. Inside the *Alice* books, love seems to have no better prospect for survival than do any of the other admirable motives and principles that underlie and make our world go round, and that fall so easily to cool Carrollian wit and satire in the nonsensical madhouses of Dodgson's invention.

The quest structures of the *Alices* offer graphic representations of a failed search for the warm joy and security of love. Once inside Wonderland, Alice desperately seeks to enter the "loveliest garden you ever saw" — that is, for almost everyone in Carroll's original audience, the Garden of Eden. But instead of a tranquil, secluded place of perfect love, the Queen of Hearts' Croquet Grounds turn out to be the grounds for perfect (albeit laughable) hate and fury — like a comic Blakean Garden of Love, an ironically perverted, dreadfully confused and threatening version of the paradise the child in us seeks in its joys and desires. In *Through the Looking-Glass* — a very different sort of book and one containing several positive but fleeting images of love — Alice's quest for Queenhood does not meet with exactly the same frustration, although it too ends in "dreadful confusion" which Alice must escape because she "ca'n't stand [it] any longer!"

In any case, being a Queen, Alice discovers, offers neither the security of attachment nor the sovereignty of freedom to which she refers in her opening words to the White Knight: "I don't want to be anybody's prisoner. I want to be a Queen." Finally, then, Alice's worlds under the ground and inside the mirror turn out, it seems, to be nonsensical places without love, places of sheer and terrifying loneliness: in both, Alice cries bitter tears engendered by that loneliness. "I am so *very* tired of being all alone here!" she sobs in Wonderland; and with a "melancholy voice" behind the looking glass, she cries, "it is so *very* lonely here!"

These apparent contradictions between text and context and within the text itself raise some important critical questions, among them these: Why, in view of Carroll's declared purposes for his *Alice* books and in view of other, abundant evidence (literary, historical, and biographical), do the *Alice* narratives seem to frustrate all impulses towards love—even the impulses their own frames excite? Why does love within the *Alices* exist, apparently, only fitfully and only in self-centered, infantile forms or in places where, so to speak, things have no names? More specifically, how can these beloved masterpieces of our literature be surrounded by so many frames of human love and yet apparently exclude love from their central stories? Finally, why do adult readers today often remember the *Alices*, despite all this evidence to the contrary, as somehow warm, even loving, experiences and Alice herself as the embodiment of Dodgson's own later vision of her:

> What wert thou, dream-Alice, in thy foster-father's eyes? How shall he picture thee? Loving, first, loving and gentle: loving as a dog (forgive the prosaic simile, but I know no earthly love so pure and perfect), and gentle as a fawn.

II

Elizabeth Sewell's celebrated study of Carroll and Lear, *The Field of Nonsense*, explains why love has no place in nonsense, why, indeed, love and nonsense are ultimately incompatible. Basically, Sewell's argument rests on the firm premise that nonsense is game; consequently, *Alice in Wonderland* and *Through the Looking-Glass* for Sewell, eminent examples of English nonsense) must turn all life, all fluid human emotions, everything, into cold, discrete, static counters for play within a closed field. The nonsense world inside the *Alices*, claims Sewell, "is not a universe of things but of words and ways of using them, plus a certain amount of pictorial illustrations. . . . In Nonsense all the world is paper and all the seas are ink."

Bearing in mind that the games in Carroll's *Alices* often involve kinetic, changing counters, rather than the static ones required for the game of nonsense postulated by Sewell (and accepted by diverse critics as an apt description of Carroll's chief comic power); keeping in mind, for example, those wriggling, live-animal mallets and live-animal balls of Wonderland croquet, we can nevertheless pursue Sewell's argument profitably. For her, the *Alices* constitute, finally, "a work about itself." Thus, love—whether as a serious subject or as a substantial conceptual element with more than mere game-counter applications, or as the spirit (style, tone, manner, etc.) in which the game of nonsense is played—has no place whatsoever in, indeed is destructive of, the game world we must enter when we enter the non-referential worlds of, say Lear's poetry or "Jabberwocky." For what we understand by human love (unlike, incidentally, Dodgson's "pure and perfect" love of dog or of fawn) is fiercely kinetic, its kinesis and imperfection dominating the subject matter of Western literature since at least the Renaissance. Furthermore, human love never is (as every game counter must be) completely discrete, never fully completed, never isolated, and never merely about itself. Indeed, the Romantic sensibility in which so many of us agonize and glory depends heavily on the principle of incompleteness and on dreams of mergers between ordinarily discrete entities and selves (in our day represented most often by sexual unions; in Carroll's day represented most vividly in the operatic vision of love celebrated in Romantic fictions, *Wuthering Heights* being a striking example). A game uses separate entities as playthings; love, like imagination, seeks to dissolve separation and to engender syntheses greater than the sums of their parts (according to Sewell, "The Nonsense universe must be the sum of its parts and nothing more").

Thus, accepting Sewell's definition, we must understand love as in a sense destructive of nonsense, as the warm emotional force that naturally resists taking the world the way nonsense presumably takes it, as simply a congeries of cold, discrete "units going one and one and one." Love works like a solvent, dissolving isolation and breaking down separateness, making the world more fluid and less static, tending towards fusion and away from discreteness. Therefore, our quest for love in the nonsensical *Alices*, like Alice's nonsensical quest for the tranquil innocence of the lovely Garden or for the permanent freedom of adult Queenhood, seems therefore nonsensical too and appropriately destined to fail. Hence it appears that, as critics anyway, we must simply declare that the warm (and sometimes sentimental) love which permeates the frame materials of the *Alices* and which is sometimes ridiculed within their narratives has no place there, is finally extraneous, playing no important part in the books' artistic successes. In fact, it looks as though we must as critics declare the few bits of unsatiric or unsatirized love we catch here and there in the *Alices* to be sentimentally generated flaws in the generally pure nonsense which is their principal achievement.

A useful gloss on these matters appears in one of Carroll's minor early fictions, "Novelty and Romancement" (published in *The Train* in 1856 when Dodgson was twenty-four and just getting used to his new pen-name). In brief, "Novelty and Romancement" is the first-person account of one Leopold Edgar Stubbs (among other things, a caricature of an overly Romantic narrator-hero in Poe's fiction), a young man with a feverish imagination and an all-consuming "thirst and passion . . . for poetry, for beauty, for novelty, for romancement."

The target of rather crude Carrollian derision, a Romantic mercilessly lampooned by Carroll's anti-Romantic irony, Stubbs serves as an objective correlative for the spirit motivating the Romantic quest—the foolish, almost nonsensical young lover foolishly in love with love itself. And the cream of Carroll's rather facile jest depends on Stubbs's dim-witted belief that the "romancement" he so ardently seeks (compare here Alice's two quests or the hunting of the Snark) is to be found, simply, in a mechanic's shop on Great Wattles-street: he spies the sign "Simon Lubkin. Dealer in Romancement" and thinks he has found the dear object of his life-long quest. "Romancement" (here read "Love"), he fondly believes, can be bought like herring or glue from a working-class shopman.

The climax of "Novelty and Romancement" comes when Stubbs, "with a throbbing and expectant heart," discovers that he has been "deluded by a heated imagination": he has, in his youthful ardor, misread the shopkeeper's sign (this short story, by the way, offers a treasure trove for our current school of semioticians). What he had read on the sign as "Romancement" was, all along, merely "Roman cement." Until the climax, he had never seen the "hideous gap" yawning between the "N" and the "C," "making it not one word but two!" Instead of the fused and fusing "romancement" Stubbs has hotly sought, he finds only "Roman cement," as cold and mundane a conception as the two discrete terms used to signify it (again compare the disappointing un-romantic conclusions and the awakenings to a dull reality that end Alice's dreams and quests). Stubbs is obviously from beginning to end a Romantic fool; but his "phantom hope" for "romancement," the childish dream he held with an "expectant heart," is no more foolish than is the dream-Alice that haunted Dodgson "phantomwise," or the imaginative dream-quests that motivated Alice herself—or the object of warm love any one of us might cherish in a young and hopeful imagination. Before Stubbs discovers the sad truth, Lubkin innocently tells him what the stuff in his shop is used for: "It would piece a most anything together." Stubbs of course misunderstands Lubkin's straightforward remark, thinking it refers to the spirit of "romancement," a spirit, he imagines, that "serves to connect the broken threads of human destiny"—a view of human love consistent with much that Dodgson wrote in many of his letters, diary entries and imaginative works, a view of human love (and the imagination) to which most of us post-Romantics probably would subscribe.

In any case, the emotional-imaginative cement fusing the two separate, lifeless, prosaic terms in Stubbs's poetic and "fertile imagination" suddenly loses its cohesive powers and its own fertility; the frigid, isolated words fly apart into mere individual words again, mere dead counters in the unimaginative game of commerce and commercial communication. The experienced Stubbs puts it neatly at the end, without for once his florid and poetic prose, "the dream was over." Like a reversed mirror-image of the ends of Alice's dream-quests, like the apparent relationships between the poetic, Romantic frames of the *Alices* and their satirical and nonsensical prose narratives, this ending seems to deflate love into a mere misreading of lifeless signs. As it so often does in Carroll, Romanticism here becomes a matter of poor eyesight. The coherent, unitary vision of a coherent, dynamic world alive and turning on the power of love is shattered into the dreadful but business-like perception of a "real" world of "broken threads" that goes round because each separate entity and each separate word remains separate, minding its "own business," while each seeker of love's coherence remains a fool permanently isolated in a solitary and loveless prison.

Preposterous as it might seem, then, we find ourselves at this point apparently forced by firm and varied evidence to conclude that the supreme and loving creations of a man whose life and religious devotion circled around love have themselves internally little to do with love — except to treat it where it occurs with the same cold mockery they turn on all the other fond fictions and groundless imaginative constructs that help make our mad world livable. Our quest for love inside these texts seems therefore doomed to the fate suffered by similar quests within Carroll's masterpieces: whether we seek it with care and hope or with thimbles and forks, love will, Carroll's great fantasies seem to say, elude us forever. The old signs, the old words declaring love's fusing magic, like the words on Simon Lubkin's sign proclaiming his prosaic wares, fall before our clear vision into their morally meaningless, discrete parts. "Novelty and Romancement" ends both sadly and comically:

The signboard yet creaks upon the moldering wall, but its sound
shall make music in these ears nevermore — ah! nevermore.

III

But our quest for the sustained and sustaining music of love within the *Alices* need not end with a frustrating Boojum. In the eighth chapter of *Through the Looking-Glass* ("It's My Own Invention"), that quest yields some authentic results. And, in spite of the apparent incoherent randomness of Carroll's nonsense materials, this chapter might even suggest for the *Alices* the possibility of a satisfying moral shape.

Besides finding in "It's My Own Invention" some of the best evidence of the loving nature that Dodgson claimed was Alice in Wonderland's chief virtue, we witness in this late, concluding episode something which, in terms of our own search for love, is much more significant — a response to that loving nature in the only genuine, fully human exchange within all of Alice's adventures: a poignantly brief, disturbingly realistic farewell between a foolish old White Knight and Alice, that Knight's beloved seven-and-a-half-year-old maiden in distress.

At this late and pivotal point in her adventures underground and behind the looking glass, Carroll's imprisoned pawn-princess is freed and is now about to awaken to autonomous Queenhood (chapter 9 is called simply "Queen Alice"). Meanwhile, Alice's thinly disguised creator Carroll/Dodgson (after surreptitiously admitting that she too is his "own invention") prepares to lose forever his Galatea as she races off eagerly and unthinkingly to adulthood and out of the dream worlds he has lovingly invented for her, worlds where real death seems almost a stranger and where her natural aging process has been slyly slowed to a Wonderland rate closer to his heart's desire — a mere half-year's maturation for something like every nine years on the other side of the looking-glass. Carroll's sadly ineffectual persona, meantime, that aged and impotent prince-charming, that familiar nonsense-inventor, the ever-falling, pitiable White Knight, sings his last song and bumbles off towards some isolated and ridiculous death:

> As the Knight sang the last words of the ballad, he gathered up the reins, and turned his horse's head along the road by which they had come. "You've only a few yards to go," he said, "down the hill and over that little brook, and then you'll be a Queen — But you'll stay and see me off first?" he added as Alice turned with an eager look in the direction to which he pointed. "I sha'n't be long. You'll wait and wave your handkerchief when I get to that turn in the road? I think it'll encourage me, you see."

In this chapter, Carroll finally brings to the surface and objectifies for his readers what they have at best only dimly sensed in their journeys with Alice through the loveless realms of heartless queens and unfeeling flat characters from the worlds of nonsense game and nursery rhyme. Until now, the only possible evidence of real love, it seemed, had been so deeply embedded among the nonsense adventures that we could have easily called *lovelessness* the keynote of the *Alices*. Until this late chapter of Carroll's last *Alice*, it appeared as if the only cogent and critically defensible way for us to justify continuing our quest for love

was to claim perhaps that the narrative act itself—the narrator's gentle structur-
ing of the inherently unstructurable, separate, discrete components of Alice's
dreams into a pleasurably coherent text—comprises an act of love, a love-gift
that provides Alice and the reader with a fictive shape which allows them to sur-
vive with some measure of sanity in a mad world. But this seems to me an un-
satisfying, overly theoretical approach to our actual experience of the *Alices*.
Now, however, in the poignant passage I have just quoted, we begin to see some
reason to hope for real success in our quest.

But before continuing, let us turn for a moment to Carroll's prefatory
poem, specifically to a passage that promises a particular emotional immunity.
The poem ends:

> And, though the shadow of a sigh
>   May tremble through the story,
> For "happy summer days" gone by,
>   And vanish'd summer glory—
> It shall not touch, with breath of bale,
> The pleasance of our fairy-tale.

The narrative following this promise, however, fails to sustain such an emotional
immunity. Indeed, the emotional charge underlying the haunting farewell between the White Knight and Alice is so powerful it breaks through the neat nonsense surfaces of Alice's adventures, letting readers and listeners hear distinctly
and directly a different but vaguely familiar tone—that nostalgic "shadow of a
sigh" which, though we hardly suspected it, has, as Carroll admits, "tremble[d]
through the story" ever since Alice first followed Dodgson's White Rabbit down
the rabbit-hole.

The intrusion of such a nostalgic "sigh" subverts Carroll's own intention to
give his audience a love-gift of game-like, pure, nonsensical pleasure untouched
alike by any breath of "bale" or by any warm, fluid emotions that can threaten
the static discreteness upon which the "pleasance" of nonsense games rests. (In
Dodgson's day, incidentally, "pleasance" signified, among other things, [1] a
pleasant, unthreatening emotional experience, [2] for him, Alice Pleasance Liddell, his real girl-love, and [3], a secluded garden.) Admitting to the field of
nonsense an emotion as alien as nostalgia risks opening its pleasant seclusion to
other disturbing strangers, among them Death. Here in chapter 8, Death is no
longer a stranger, a separate word, a mere uncharged sign and discrete counter
for endless games where "they never executes nobody" and where Death's agent
Time can itself die, or stop dead forever in a mad, unending tea-party. And the
"voice of dread" that, as Carroll's poem reminds us, inevitably "summon[s] to
unwelcome bed" every "melancholy maiden" here also breaks through, becoming

fully manifest for the only time in all the adventures, but thereby revealing it has been a dynamic element singing at the back of Carroll's tales of Alice's nonsensical experiences of life, love, death and disorder.

Carroll himself understood the threat such a "breath of bale" poses for nonsense games. Consciously, he believed that the approaching, inexorable "bedtime" his poem alludes to must not, would not play any part in the adventures themselves (except heavily disguised in such elements as the many silly and unthreatening death and sex jokes that punctuate the *Alices*). But here in "It's My Own Invention"—the chapter Carroll apparently considered central to the book (look at that frontispiece again)—the baleful "frost," the "raving blast" of fall and winter which is our common lot and the basis for much of our love comes alive dramatically in the comic narrative's overt and realistic portrayals of aging, old age, and falling to earth (the text alludes to the old Knight's falling at least thirty times), as well as in its covert plays on the word "grave" and its many references to gravity—a no-nonsense, inescapable force pulling us all down to earth and our common grave. And the tone that conveys all this, the emotional aura suffusing this autumnal scene which reaches its climax with the spectacle of an aged man (not a mere nonsense creature, mind you, but a *man*) singing, as his final love-gift for a departing child, his nonsense song "The Aged Aged Man," that melancholy tone we hear distinctly in "It's My Own Invention" reveals, finally and with a direct immediacy, a fundamental thematic element that has subtly informed all of the *Alice* books, making them something much more referential, much richer and more human than the insulated nonsense we might have easily mistaken them for. Paradoxically, this grave tone emanates from Carroll's fortunate failure to keep his nonsense pure, free from that "shadow of a sigh" he himself admits. The tone emanates from a deep, abiding and inescapable sense that human love springs from time and human mortality. Hardly a fit subject for the closed fields of nonsense, but just the right subject for literary works quoted as often as Shakespeare's sonnets.

Much of the love Dodgson bore for the innumerable little Alices of his own fleeting life was of a kind adult readers know well. His letters and diaries (and his lesser literary works) are fully open about that sense of advancing age that leaves us fallen "bare ruined choirs" and makes us "love that well which [we] must leave ere long." The depth and intensity of Dodgson's preoccupation with this particular emotional and spiritual experience can be gauged by the heavy emphasis placed upon it in this structurally crucial chapter, especially in the chapter's continual iteration of two intertwined motifs—old age and falling. Like Shakespeare's May-time beloved beholding the final decline of a wintertime lover, like Humbert Humbert's pitiful adoration of his indifferent nymphet fading before him into a future he cannot share, like any of the countless

figures in our literature that dramatize and celebrate this notion of love springing from fallen man's doomed race against world and time, against the impris-
oning Biological Trap or the "blight man was born for," the *Alice* undertexts,
amidst all the surface nonsense, have whispered from the beginning of love's intimate relations with inevitable death, but so faintly and subtly that the effect is
necessarily—and, I think, appropriately—subliminal. In this late, sunset
chapter of the final *Alice*, however, in this autumnal and peculiarly isolated
scene of final parting between (foster) father and the child he has created, the
grave undercurrent themes of age, evanescent and unrequited love and youth's
impatience for autonomous life become for a very brief moment the vivid mainstream and audible melody of Carroll's narrative.

Indeed, we now know that Carroll intended to intensify these themes and
make them even more explicit in this chapter: With a characteristic *Looking-
Glass* doubling, he meant (although he was finally dissuaded by Tenniel) to add
immediately after the White Knight episode a parallel scene of young Alice
parting from another aged man—the even older, dying Wasp in a Wig, who
sings a sometimes gruesome song about his own last days:

> So now that I am old and gray,
>   And all my hair is nearly gone,
> They take my wig from me and say
>   "How can you put such rubbish on?"

But although the Wasp episode does bear a number of similarities to the
White Knight section it was meant to follow, it might not appear to be about love,
the goal of our own critical quest. For while the "*very* unhappy" Wasp represents
the sadness of approaching death (being November behind the looking-glass, it is
already well past the "unwelcome bedtime" of most wasps) and while Alice again
represents impatient youth (she turns back to the aged Wasp "rather unwillingly,
for she was *very* anxious to be a Queen"), readers might nevertheless find it difficult to discover in this Wasp fragment any hint of the love-out-of-death theme I
have been delineating. But the distinct change Alice's polite indulgence effects in
this irascible old creature should be read in the light of its full context, representing as it does the sudden engendering of warm human emotion in the coldest,
most rigid and elderly figure in Carroll's extensive collection of cranky, inflexible,
waspish grown-ups. In the final words of this episode, the Wasp suddenly reaches
emotionally towards Alice, displaying some true civility—a delicate social sign
that for fastidious Dodgson sometimes conveyed private love:

> "Good-bye, and thank-ye," said the Wasp, and Alice tripped
> down the hill again, quite pleased that she had gone back and given
> a few minutes to making the poor old creature comfortable.

Such genuine civility—here in response to Alice's acts of genuine noblesse oblige for a "poor creature" of the lower orders (lower biologically, socially, morally)—coming so spontaneously and from such an improbable source, represents, I think, the miraculous regenerative power loving childhood offers to the dying old: a spiritual solvent that can teach us to love and can free us from our emotional and class-conscious rigidity and isolation, as it so often freed Charles Dodgson from his.

In any case, Lewis Carroll's concentration on his peculiar child-love version of the eros-thanatos principle, his bitter-sweet and sentimental vision of a fallen old man's innocent and fruitless love for an even more innocent, unattainable child, shapes many features of "It's My Own Invention." And comprehending Carroll's strategies for transforming that vision into the nonsensical parting of a ludicrous White Knight and an eager Alice—a parting that also comically announces the approaching end of his *Alices* and the approaching end of their loving inventor—will allow us to understand better the love in the *Alices*.

For one thing, "It's My Own Invention" dramatizes a strikingly realistic encounter between two human figures as familiar in literary convention as they are in ordinary life—the aged, inept, foolish and sometimes doting lover and the indifferent, impatient, lively young object of his love. Carroll naturally employs several screens, and his treatment of this traditional material differs widely from the standard comic and tragic sentimentality with which his audience was most familiar. But many of the principal elements of the convention operate in Carroll's nonsense rendition. For example, what is often emphasized in such a couple (for tragic as well as for comic purposes) is their essential incompatibility. Here that incompatibility is deftly underscored and elaborated in some noteworthy ways. Alice, for instance, looks upon the aged Knight as a laughable old fool, but she takes pains to conceal her youthful amusement and "dares not laugh" at him; she generously allows him to mistake her "puzzled" thoughts about his ridiculous invention of a Platonic pudding for "sad" thoughts about her eagerly awaited departure. The Knight, for his part, considers his sentimental and funny song beautifully sad, while, upon hearing it, Alice finds "no tears [come] into her eyes," and even he is forced to observe gently that she did not cry as much as he thought she would. From all of this emerges a subtle, curious emotional exchange, a kind of loving mutuality we have not seen directly before in the adventures and one that, on Alice's side, represents far more than just her well-bred politeness. The fleeting love that whispers through this scene is, therefore, complex and paradoxical; it is a love between a child all potential, freedom, flux and growing up and a man all impotence, imprisonment, stasis and falling down.

While the White Knight's continual falling and his outlandish horsemanship also suggest sexual impotence (his name, it should be noted, constitutes a pun on a familiar term for a sleepless night — a "white night" — in the context of these great dream books itself a mark of stasis and impotence, as well as a reference to the kinetic, waking world of love and mortality that keeps breaking through this chapter), that falling bears a more immediate and wider reference to other sharp contrasts between him and Alice, who has now attained the evanescent ability to handle, with the grace of childhood, some rather tricky matters of gravity and balance. Indeed, some of the conversation here sounds as if Alice is now the knowing grown-up and the Knight the innocent child (a role reversal mirrored in a number of *Looking-Glass* and *Wonderland* episodes). Considering his propensity for falling, for example, Alice at one point declares, "You ought to have a wooden horse on wheels, that you ought!" and he sheepishly asks, "Does that kind go smoothly?" It is this sort of second-childhood childishness, his near-senile frailty and dependence on a fickle child, that makes him here laughable and pitiable at the same time (surely an undesirable fusion in the game of nonsense). And it is the utter hopelessness of his attachment to the departing child that, I submit, makes him a haunting figure of universal reference.

When the Knight, "a faint smile lighting up his gentle foolish face," sings his parting song for Alice, adult readers might easily overlook, in all its silly nonsense, the serious, common-sensical aspects of the song and of the entire scene. But the child Alice is not nearly so insensitive — she somehow grasps the episode's strange gravity:

> Of all the strange things that Alice saw in her journey Through The Looking-Glass, this was the one that she always remembered most clearly. Years afterwards she could bring the whole scene back again, as if it had been only yesterday — the mild blue eyes and kindly smile of the Knight — the setting sun gleaming through his hair . . . and the black shadows of the forest behind — all this she took in like a picture . . . listening, in a half-dream, to the melancholy music of the song.

For the open-hearted Alice has unwittingly heard the poignant, hopeless love of The Aged Aged Man that moves secretly beneath the song's surface nonsense. And, as Carroll subtly suggests, there is a reasonable chance that Alice Liddell (in her own "half-dream," halfway between her actual, listening, reading, waking self and her fantasy self inside the dream-fiction) has heard similarly that same melancholy music here and there throughout the nonsensical adventures — Dodgson's trembling, grave "shadow of a sigh" that makes Carroll's best nonsense books timeless and universal in ways far beyond the capacity of mere unreferential nonsense.

The tune of "The Aged Aged Man," as Alice says to herself, "*isn't* his own invention" as he claims; the tune (and Alice apparently identifies its source correctly) comes from Thomas Moore's "My Heart and Lute," a poignant love lyric that no seven-and-a-half-year-old could completely understand. As Martin Gardner suggests, "It is quite possible that Carroll regarded Moore's love lyric as the song that he, the White Knight [and Charles Lutwidge Dodgson], would have liked to sing to Alice [and to Alice Pleasance Liddell] but dared not." In any case, Alice's politely unspoken recognition of the underlying love lyric here bespeaks her acute child's ear, her high-bred diplomacy, and her precocious sensitivity to the oblique voice of love beneath the nonsense of his song and, I submit, beneath all her fantastic adventures.

If we join Alice in recognizing such a faint but powerful loving counterpoint, we add a new dimension to our understanding of the *Alices*. Moore's song begins, "I give thee all — I can no more — / Though poor the off'ring be. / My heart and lute are all the store / That I can bring to thee." The White Knight's song, in turn, is also a poor offering, like the many poor nonsensical offerings of another aged and silly inventor, given also in tones of modest love to an unattainable child impatient for life and ultimately incapable of understanding the pathetic depth of such grown-up melancholy music. Moore's singer sings of a "soul of love" and a "heart that feels / Much more than lute could tell." Carroll's nonsense music likewise cannot — must not — tell fully what Dodgson's heart feels. Alice, of course, while capable of recognizing the poignant love song beneath the nonsense words, is, ironically, blessedly incapable of understanding fully what that curious blend of words and music tells about herself, about the old man singing before her and about the human condition: "She stood and listened very attentively, but no tears came into her eyes." Fortunately, only adults can hear, if they listen very attentively, all of Carroll's gravity and melancholy love. Only adults can hear the full sad irony, for example, of this little nonsensical exchange between innocent Alice and her experienced White Knight:

> "People don't fall off quite so often, when they've had much practice."

> "I've had plenty of practice," the Knight said very gravely: "plenty of practice!"

Before leaving this discussion of the melancholy tone of love upon which Carroll's nonsense tales are based, we should remind ourselves that the oral element, the sound of the human voice (particularly, the spoken words of a wise and kindly, upper-middle-class Oxford don, the product of Christ Church, Rugby, and a well-bred family) can play a major, critically legitimate role in our assessments of the *Alices*. The fact that Alice and her original adventures grew out of their inventor's extemporaneous, oral story-telling seems to me important.

And when we add to this the fact that references to the literal occasion for the first telling of *Under Ground* whisper here and there through the texts themselves (the last words of *Looking-Glass*, for example, take us suddenly back twenty years to a boat-full of real Liddells eagerly and with "willing ear" waiting "to hear" Dodgson's "simple tale"), we can probably assume that Carroll wrote all three *Alices* with the sounds of the human voice constantly and vividly in mind. That assumption becomes a critical certainty when we comprehend the extent and importance of Carroll's countless stage and musical directions—here say it "gravely" (seriously and with full knowledge of the grave); there say it with "a scream of laughter." These directions can serve of course as oral performance notes for a grown-up storyteller as much as they can serve as simple modifiers for imaginative silent readers, be they adults or children. And such matters deserve careful investigation.

But such an investigation must wait for another occasion. Suffice it to say that the sense of a stable, orderly and correct voice (without the stammer from which Dodgson often suffered when talking to most adults), speaking in calm tones, and with great sympathy for its child subject and for its child audience, informs the *Alices*, guiding our responses, fusing and shaping the discrete nonsense materials with a warm and consistently loving tone. Many readers of the *Alices* today probably hear, consciously or not, that voice of love beneath the silly adventures, like the Moore love lyric beneath the nonsense song "The Aged Aged Man." And for those who do hear, that voice somehow humanizes Carroll's games of nonsense, making the whole *Alice* experience into a love-gift as worthy of the childlike teller as it has been of his countless childlike listeners ever since.

"And here I must leave you. . . . You are sad," says the White Knight to Alice; but "in an anxious tone" he adds, "let me sing you a song to comfort you." No one else in Alice's many adventures has ever addressed her quite this way. It is as if the narrator and the narrator's gentle, loving voice have crossed over some boundary between reality and fiction, between Alice's adventures and Carroll's telling of them. It is the White Knight Carroll's last farewell and last love-gift to his beloved invention Alice. After this he must, like his inventor Dodgson (who has had plenty of sad practice saying good-bye to real girls entering queenhood), continue his well-practiced falling, alone and unaided to the end. In his later years Dodgson writes to a former girl friend now about to enter the dubious queenhood of Victorian marriage:

> My child-friends are all marrying off, now, terribly quick! But, for a solitary broken-hearted old bachelor, it is certainly soothing to find that some of them, even when engaged, continue to write as "yours affectionately"! But for that, you will easily perceive that my solitude would be simply desperate!

"Desperate" is perhaps too strong a word here — certainly too strong for a Victorian clergyman like Dodgson, and probably too strong to describe the White Knight's own parting words and song. But "desperate" is not so wide of the mark: both Alice and the Knight, after all, recognize that "the Aged Aged Man" is full of very "melancholy music." And, in many senses, so is the nonsensical chapter that contains it. For the impending loneliness, the approaching loss of love and life for which both Dodgson and his "anxious" White Knight have been practicing so long in their inventive imaginations, is far from a laughing matter. It is serious enough to make them both seek soothing comfort and faint hope in the merest crumbs of affection from a loving child's fickle heart.

IV

Carroll's doomed attempts to keep his beloved child-friends forever "dreaming as the summers die," his brilliant deployment of "magic words" to "hold [them] fast," his perfectly composed photographs that try to fix them forever in their passing youth — all these things represent a glorious and futile struggle of loving art against separating Time, that most abused and ridiculed figure of Carroll's many fantasies. In "It's My Own Invention," Time is finally displayed openly in its full relation to the human condition, a relation usually well masked by Carroll's sprightly nonsense. Here Carroll's many allusions to Time in the *Alices* and elsewhere seem to come into sharp emotional and moral focus, offering suddenly a brief but clear and feeling vision of Time's human significance — the despised irresistible agent of our ludicrous mortality and our wonderful love.

Nearing fifty, Dodgson writes in a letter to an adult friend, "the experience of many years [has] taught me that there are few things in the world so evanescent as a child's love." And because the poignantly familiar love of an aged man for a young and innocent child intensifies that evanescence several-fold, it serves as a fine symbol (in literary fantasies as well as in everyday psychology) for the evanescence and preciousness of all love and of life itself. Thus, the terribly brief encounter between a child about to experience for the first time "queenhood" and its concomitant knowledge of death's "unwelcome bed" and a loving, protecting but foolish adult who has had "plenty of practice" — that evanescent moment permanently stopped by art's saving magic — should be understood as Carroll's special message to us, his fellow grown-ups: his own, covert interpretation, if you will, of the *Alices*, an interpretation at least as graphic as the frontispiece he chose, presumably, to depict their central theme of youth and age.

Essentially, the *Alices* stop time in their surface nonsense, presenting to the child in their readers and listeners an unthreatened and unthreatening vista of seemingly endless play, play (like the Caucus Race or Tweedle brothers' battle) curiously, charmingly static and full of discrete counters within a safe, closed field. But for their adult audience they give something more: they also whisper some sad truths about the world of flux beyond that pleasant field. The walls of Carroll's nonsense are thus constantly, if surreptitiously, breached by Time and Death and consequently, as I have argued here, by the love that springs from them both. So while Carroll's love-gift of the *Alices* helps the child Alice "keep, through all her riper years, the simple and loving heart of her childhood," another voice sings softly at the same time to other ears, to those for whom childhood's dreams might already be like a "pilgrim's wither'd wreath of flowers / Pluck'd in a far-off land."

Because it breaks open the closed field of nonsense with love, we can say that Carroll's finest comedy is much better than the cool nonsense he is often credited with. Better because it is about much more than mere nonsense is about; better because it takes account of a familiar human world charged with love and fear of death. And better because it is, finally, morally superior to the most elegantly cerebral nonsense, telling us fellow humans, in tones of love, truths about our nature in a manner that somehow makes delight of our foibles and lovely, evanescent joys of our sorrows. Like so much Victorian comedy from Carlyle and Dickens to Eliot and Meredith, Carroll's *Alices* are great and good because they rest finally upon the warm, fusing morality and sentiment the Victorian age cherished as "humor" — not upon those surface games which have brought Carroll so much critical esteem in recent years, but which his own age probably would have considered mere entertaining "wit."

Therefore, Carroll is for yet another reason one of our best writers of subversive comedy, this time because of his treatment of love. Like his satire, his witty nonsense often subverts love and sentimentality; of this we are all well aware. But in addition, as we might not have noticed, his love subverts his nonsense and satire. In this Carrollian world of mixed-up signs and sensibilities, the question, as one of Carroll's most unloving characters would say, is "which is to be master — that's all." Dodgson, probably, would have chosen love and romance as the masters of nonsense. The more important question of whether or not Carroll would have made the same choice can be answered in only one place, the *Alices* themselves. And these, wonderful adventures seem to tell us, finally, that there is no need for any masters here; indeed, neither nonsense, nor death, nor love can master the rich, fused music of all three that makes the peculiar, abiding romancement of the *Alices* so delightfully complex.

POSTSCRIPT

"unless this miracle have might"

Carroll probably had the last word, so to speak, on these matters of nonsense, referentiality, time, death and love in his *Alices*—not exactly in a word, but in a picture. The last words of *Alice's Adventures under Ground* (and of *Alice's Adventures in Wonderland*, too) are these: ". . . remembering her own child-life, and the happy summer days." But between those last two discrete but resonating terms "summer" and "days," at the very end of the *Under Ground* manuscript sits Carroll's referent herself, the real dream-child Dodgson really loved, the real Alice Liddell gazing from her own "summer days"—out of the 1860s and Dodgson's lovely photograph and right into our eyes.

Although this little picture was meant for Alice's eyes alone, it still can play an important part in our understanding of love and death in Carroll's *Alices*. For in this haunting photograph of Alice—set into the beautifully hand-wrought, illustrated *Alice* text and joining (as well as separating) those two, final, discrete words—Carroll embodies the motives and issues that first stirred his heart to create the nonsensical *Alices* and to animate them with a special, curious melancholy music beyond the reach of nonsense. Here before our eyes, then, is his sensitive portrait of the child who is both his heroine and his beloved audience; both a creature in his fictional texts and a real child living outside them; both a thing fashioned from mere words and the living vessel for the "loving heart of childhood." Before us is the actual little recipient of a very precious love-gift, the only copy of one of the world's greatest fictions. Through the loving devotion of a brilliant and meticulous photographer, Alice here somehow defies Time—as if some mad inventor from Alice's dream worlds had, with the magic of his words and art, found a way in her waking world to defy gravity and stop aging and death by means of an improbable Wonderland light-machine and some Looking-Glass Roman-cement.

The *Under Ground* photograph records one discrete moment in the actual life of one discrete child. Moreoever, it records that moment without recourse to an inevitably generalizing verbal medium (even the precious name "Alice" is a name many can share). In the wood where things have no names, Alice seems to find, for a moment, the elusive love she seeks. Here in this picture of his beloved Alice, Carroll pierces through his own verbal medium to a place beyond names and beyond art, bringing into his text life itself and, in a real sense, the love we all seek—embodied in one specific, very real little girl. In my mind, then, whatever else Alice's *Under Ground* photograph tells us, it certainly speaks the last word about nonsense, referentiality, time, death and love in Carroll's *Alices*.

BEVERLY LYON CLARK

Carroll's Well-Versed Narrative: Through the Looking-Glass

You say that I'm "to write a verse"—
O Maggie, put it quite
The other way, and kindly say
That I'm "averse to write"!

In writing to his child-friends Lewis Carroll was not averse to verse, however he might tease. Nor was he averse in his fiction—for it comprises one of the most memorable features of his *Alice* books. It contributes to the humor and non-sense and absurdity of the books, through its play with "real"-world forms and its parody, and through its concreteness and its interaction with the surrounding prose.

Carroll played with "real"-world forms sometimes by making things more orderly and sometimes by making them less. But of course order and disorder are all a matter of perspective. When Humpty Dumpty defines glory as "a nice knock-down argument" he disorders our real-world semantic order, from one perspective, but the simple act of defining the word, of associating it with a meaning and not leaving it in the limbo of meaningless noises, is itself an act of order. Humpty Dumpty's new order may be unfamiliar, but it is not entirely chaotic. Or take "Jabberwocky." Does it disorder our orderly universe? Yes, in part, for "brillig" and "slithy" have no familiar meaning. Yet, as students of language are fond of pointing out, the grammatical structure of the poem is orderly, making it possible for us to decipher, for instance, the parts of speech

From *English Language Notes* 20, no. 2 (December 1982). © 1982 by the Regents of the University of Colorado.

to which the nonsense words belong. And the words themselves combine consonants and vowels the way English words do (unlike, say, the Wonderland Gryphon's "Hjckrrh!"). Further, Humpty Dumpty's explication provides an ordering of the meaning as well. When he expounds, "'*Brillig*' means four o'clock in the afternoon—the time when you begin *broiling* things for dinner," he describes a world with a modicum of order, one that can be envisioned as in, say, Tenniel's drawing.

Another way of describing Carroll's play with "real"-world forms is in terms of open and closed fields. Susan Stewart, in her recent study *Nonsense*, catalogues nonsense transformations and finds some within the closed fields described by Elizabeth Sewell in her early *Field of Nonsense*, closing what is traditionally open, while others do the inverse, opening what is closed. Yet whatever we call the two transformations—whether we use this broad definition or else associate the second with the absurd—Carroll uses both kinds. He sometimes opens what is traditionally closed (making a mirror into a door) and sometimes closes what is traditionally open and on-going (making time stand still at six o'clock). And often what Carroll does is a complex amalgam of both opening and closing. In his parodies, for instance, some of the wordplay focuses attention on the words, fencing them off from reality, making them a closed world: rhyme and alliteration draw attention to the words and distract us from whatever it is the words are meant to refer to. The parodies also close themselves off as separate worlds to the extent that they do not refer to recognizable reality: how does one balance anything as slippery and floppy as an eel on the end of one's nose? On the other hand, the references to artifacts outside the poems—to other poems—opens the form, and the parodies would also seem to shatter the closed universes of the pietistic poems they mock. The parodies operate in both closed and open fields—they both order and disorder—and part of their effect derives from the confrontation between the two. We can call them nonsense, or something else, but the parodies draw upon both kinds of transformation.

It has become convenient to refer offhand to most of the verse in the *Alice* books as parodies. But again we run into a problem of definition. This time I want to define the term more narrowly, for the very general way in which we use "parody" sometimes blinds us to important distinctions. Sometimes we call something a parody if it reminds us of a previous work, whether or not any satire is intended. But I'd like to reserve parody for something that satirizes. Dwight Macdonald, for instance, situates Carroll's works closer to what he calls burlesque than to parody: "he simply injected an absurd content into the original form with no intention of literary criticism." Macdonald is right for some of Carroll's verse, but I would disagree with his contention that Carroll never intended literary criticism, for sometimes Carroll does intend literary, if not moral, criticism.

Sometimes, if not always. For only in *Alice's Adventures in Wonderland* is the verse truly parodic. "*How doth the little crocodile*," for instance, undermines the pious preaching of Isaac Watts's "How doth the little busy bee," which admonishes children to keep busy and avoid mischief: the crocodile presented for our emulation, far from skillfully building a cell or neatly spreading wax, "cheerfully" and "neatly" and "gently" — snares fishes. Much of the other pious verse that Carroll parodies in *Wonderland* is similarly subverted. While Carroll does not entirely disagree with the sentiments of the poems he parodies — especially in later life, when he wanted to outbowdlerize Bowdler — and thus does not mock that which is preached, he does mock the preaching. Carroll may not be criticizing the content (he surely is not inciting children to be slothful), but he does criticize the literary purpose of didactic verse, the way in which it tried to control children. In part Carroll may simply be entering into the child's perspective, adopting the child's responses to pietistic verse, for he shows considerable sympathy for the child's point of view. And perhaps Carroll's satire of the didacticism of previous children's literature clears a niche for the new kind of children's literature he wanted to write. Much as Alice tries to define herself by attempting to recite familiar verse, Carroll seems, intentionally or not, to be defining his fiction through Alice's failure to define herself, through her mangling of her recitations.

In *Through the Looking-Glass*, however, it is as if Carroll's success with his first children's book freed him from the need to comment on what previous writers had done for, or to, children. The verse is less parodic. Although some of it plays with pre-existing poems, it is harder to label such playing parody, harder to convict it of literary criticism. Carroll's "parodies" in the two books might be placed on a continuum, from the true parodies like that of Watts to reflections of the original that are not necessarily satires (what Macdonald describes), to mere echoes that may not actually be related to a so-called original. The drinking song begot of Scott, sung at the Looking-Glass banquet, mimics some lines of the original but probably without any intent to satirize. And still farther from parody is "The Walrus and the Carpenter," which shares its meter and rhyme scheme with Thomas Hood's "The Dream of Eugene Aram" and also the discovery of an unexpected murderer, but which is not otherwise tied to the so-called original. Carroll himself wrote in a letter to his uncle, "I had no particular poem in mind. The metre is a common one, and I don't think 'Eugene Aram' suggested it more than the many other poems I have read in the same metre."

Looking-Glass verse tends toward this latter end of the continuum. Carroll here does not demolish children's verse. For the most part, he either uses fantastical nursery rhymes, which do not need to be demolished, or else he plays with adult poetry, which can perhaps be poked and prodded at but need not be so utterly crushed as the sugar-coated moralizing intended for children.

I will demonstrate how Carroll uses pre-existing verse in *Looking-Glass* by examining the changes he rings on Wordsworth's "Resolution and Independence." The White Knight's poem includes echoes of other poems—Wordsworth's "The Thorn" and Thomas Moore's "My Heart and Lute"—but I'll concentrate on "Resolution and Independence." Carroll had written an early version of his poem by 1856, and this version describes a situation fairly close to that in Wordsworth's poem: in both the narrator encounters an extremely old man upon the moor, asks his occupation, and is comforted by the exchange—although Wordsworth's narrator is comforted by the man's cheer and steadfastness, while Carroll's is comforted by the man's "kind intent / To drink my health in beer." The closest verbal echoes are in the closing lines. Wordsworth ends with "I'll think of the Leech-gatherer on the lonely moor!" and Carroll ends with "I think of that strange wanderer / Upon the lonely moor."

This echoing of concluding lines is emblematic of the relationship between the two poems. While the Watts parody starts off proclaiming the poem it twists, repeating the opening "How doth the little," as well as "Improve" and "shining" in the second line, the Wordsworth derivative waits till the conclusion for a close verbal echo. Furthermore, Carroll entirely omits all reference to the meditative early verses of Wordsworth's poem, and even changes the meter and rhyme scheme. "Upon the Lonely Moor" is simply not very close to "Resolution and Independence." And it is not that Wordsworth's lines utterly forbid parody. Surely, if he had wanted to, Carroll could have embellished "Such seemed this Man, not all alive nor dead, / Nor all asleep" by adding something like (but better than) "Nor scrubbing scones nor eating flies / Nor starting in to weep." He apparently wanted to use Wordsworth's dramatic situation as a scaffolding more than he wanted to use Wordsworth's poem as a source for parody.

The later version of Carroll's poem, the one that appears in *Looking-Glass*, is even farther from Wordsworth. The echo in the last two lines has entirely disappeared, and so has all reference to moors. Instead of situating his aged man on a romantic and evocative moor Carroll sits him on a gate. Compared to the earlier version, the nonsense is better, the parody less.

Nevertheless, Carroll himself did call the poem a parody, in a letter to his uncle—but he went on to modify his use of the term: "'Sitting on a Gate' *is* a parody, though not as to style or metre—but its plot is borrowed from Wordsworth's 'Resolution and Independence.'. . ." Carroll uses the term "parody" for lack of a better word, to describe his borrowing of the plot, or dramatic situation, his use of the poem as a scaffolding. He goes on to indicate what in Wordsworth's poem he might well like to satirize, for it is "a poem that has always amused me a good deal (though it is by no means a comic poem) by the absurd way in which the poet goes on questioning the poor old leech-gatherer, making him tell his history over and over again, and never attending to what he says. Wordsworth ends with a moral—an example I have *not* followed." Carroll uses Wordsworth's dramatic situation here, but doing so, though it may poke fun at the narrator's greater interest in his own thoughts than in human interaction, does not undermine Wordsworth's sentiments, his praise of resolution, nor his communing with nature, nor his introspection. And the final version of the poem has strayed far enough from the original that Carroll needs to stress to his uncle that it *is* a parody.

We may be too eager to find satiric comment on Wordsworth in Carroll's poem, since the convenient label for the poem is parody and that is what parody is supposed to do. But while Carroll might not mind tweaking Wordsworth's nose when he starts platitudinizing, Carroll less clearly satirizes Wordsworth than he does Watts in the crocodile poem. And in other derived poems in *Looking-Glass*, such as that sired by Scott, the original neither pedantic nor moralistic, it is even harder to find what Carroll could be satirizing. The complexity of the relationship between Carroll's and Wordsworth's poems, or Carroll's and Scott's, a relationship not easily defined by our usual interpretation of "parody," complements the complexity of Carroll's nonsense and absurdity, which both reveres and defies, both orders and disorders, both closes and opens.

Another way in which Carroll's verse is humorous and nonsensical, in addition to parodying and playing with forms from the "real" world, is through what Elizabeth Sewell calls "a careful addiction to the concrete." Instead of evoking a twinkling star and comparing it to a diamond, Carroll makes a bat twinkle like a tea-tray. Or he unites shoes, ships and sealing wax, or cabbages and kings. Yet not all of Carroll's verse is humorous in precisely this way. Some of it is less concrete and complete in itself, and part of its humor lies in how it integrates with the surrounding narrative. And since little or no attention has been paid to this other source of humor, I am going to concentrate on it at the expense of "careful concreteness." Again, as with the parodic playing with form, the humor derives from a varying tension, or confrontation, between opening and closing the verse: the concreteness and completeness tend to close it, while the integration with the narrative opens it. In *Wonderland* the King of Hearts attempts to integrate verse into the story when he uses the lines beginning *"They told me you had been to her"* as evidence of the Knave's guilt. Yet the ambiguous pronoun references in the lines invite all interpretations—and substantiate none. And the King's attempt to use this verse as evidence ironically substantiates its inadmissibility and hence underscores the disjunction between verse and story. Much of the humor of the verse derives from the use the King makes of it.

Looking-Glass verse tends to be even more integrated with the narrative. Both form and content are integrated, the latter in four ways. I will first discuss the integration of the content, and then turn to the form.

Overall, the content integrates with the prose thematically. Alice finally says, with only slight exaggeration, that the poetry was "all about fishes." (And in the context of playing with kittens, and frequently thinking about eating, it is not amiss to dream about fishes.) In addition, some of the verse relates directly to the action: the Red Queen sings a lullaby when the White Queen wants to nap; and the creatures sing toasts at the closing banquet. Some of the verse is interpreted by the characters, who thereby attempt, as it were, to accommodate the verse to the narrative: Humpty Dumpty interprets "Jabberwocky"; and even the Tweedles offer some interpretations of "The Walrus and the Carpenter." Finally, some of the verse is enacted in the story: notably, the nursery rhymes come to life.

In providing sources for Looking-Glass characters, the nursery rhymes strengthen the integration of verse and story. Much as Wonderland creatures sprout from metaphoric proverbs (except for the Queen of Hearts and company, derived in part from a nursery rhyme but also from playing cards), such Looking-Glass creatures as Humpty Dumpty and the Tweedles derive from nursery rhymes. As Roger Henkle notes, the careers of the nursery-rhyme creatures "are predetermined by the nursery rhymes about them"—they derive, in other words, from entire verse-stories, not from mere phrases. Or, even if the creatures are ignorant of their predetermining verses, Alice and the reader are not, and we see how the verse does indeed determine actions, how highly integrated verse and narrative are. In *Wonderland*, on the other hand, while the King acts as if the previous behavior of the Knave of Hearts has been described by a nursery rhyme, Alice and the reader are not convinced. The nursery rhyme does not have determining force there—it is merely posited—while nursery rhymes do affect Looking-glass world, the verse does affect the narrative: Humpty Dumpty does come crashing down.

The appearance of nursery-rhyme characters in *Looking-Glass* also makes the book self-conscious because Alice knows about the characters in the story of her adventures through knowing other stories—she is "in the ambiguous position of being a reader in a story where she meets fictitious characters and so knows all about them." This self-consciousness is somewhat different from self-consciousness in *Wonderland*. There Alice may comment that the Mouse has reached the fifth bend of the concrete poem, self-consciously commenting on the poem; but it is only the poem that she views as a literary artifact, not the creatures she encounters. Her comments underline the differences between the poem and the narrative rather than merge them. In *Looking-Glass*, though, she is self-conscious about both poems and narrative, and she even wonders if she herself is part of the Red King's dream. Although Alice may simply be playing another version of "Let's pretend" at the end, when she asks Kitty which dreamed it, her question does hint at a serious issue. And the poem that concludes *Looking-Glass*, ending as it does with *"Life, what is it but a dream?"* continues the impetus of self-consciousness. Such self-consciousness can at first remind the reader of the boundaries between fiction and reality, since the fiction proclaims its fictionality. Hence it would close the work off from reality. Yet, as Borges queries of the work within a work: "Why does it disquiet us to know that Don Quixote is a reader of the *Quixote*, and Hamlet is a spectator of *Hamlet*? I believe I have found the answer: those inversions suggest that if the characters in a story can be readers or spectators, then we, their readers or spectators, can be fictitious." The self-consciousness in *Looking-Glass* likewise hints that what appears tangible may be only a dream, that presumed realities are really fantasies, that reality is subjective. *Looking-Glass* may not be a fully self-conscious novel, one that, in Robert Alter's words, "systematically flaunts its own condition of artifice and . . . by so doing probes into the problematic relationship between real-seeming artifice and reality," but it does tend somewhat in that direction, to confound reality and fiction. Once again, though indirectly, the *Looking-Glass* verse occasions integration, integration here of the larger realms of fiction and reality. And once again, *Looking-Glass* balances closure and self-containment with openness and permeation.

Enough of metaphysics and back to the verse again: not only is the content integrated with the narrative but so is the form. Not only is there thematic continuity between verse and prose, via fishes, and not only is one sometimes an adumbration of the other—as with the Tweedles, Humpty Dumpty, and the Lion and the Unicorn—but the physical integration of the two has also increased in *Looking-Glass*. Of course, this verse, like the verse in *Wonderland*, is set off from the rest of the text by being in verse form. Yet in *Looking-Glass* the segregation of verse and prose falters. Perhaps even the railway passengers' refrain, "— — — — is worth a thousand — — — — a — — — —," is a verse more completely integrated with narrative, a verse not typographically segregated: Alice considers the refrain "like the chorus of a song."

Once more I would like to amplify the argument by examining specific examples. First I will look at the White Knight's verse and then Humpty Dumpty's, both of which merge with the surrounding narrative.

After droning on *"mumblingly and low"* with his *"so"* / *"know"* / *"slow"* rhymes, the White Knight abruptly ends his poem with *"A-sitting on a gate."* The last line provides the rhyme for "weight" so long held in abeyance, until the record needle finally came unstuck, and hence provides some closure. Yet the poem shows a tendency to continue into, merge with, the ensuing narrative. For the interminable o-rhymes, essentially paratactic, could go on forever, comic invention willing. And they make the abrupt concluding line seem tacked on, anticlimactic. This anticlimax is humorous, as Carroll wants it to be, but it also, as Barbara Herrnstein Smith might note, leaves the reader "with residual expectations." These residual expectations make the reader receptive to the possibility of an additional line or lines. And, in fact, the next words the White Knight speaks are "You've only a few yards to go" — consistent with the poem's meter and rhyme. The poem pushes beyond its physical boundaries.

Humpty Dumpty's verse likewise shows a tendency to continue into the narrative, a merging anticipated by Alice's frequent interruptions during the recitation. Some of the stanzas are as follows:

> The little fishes' answer was
> "We cannot do it, Sir, because — — —"
>
> . . .
>
> And he was very proud and stiff:
> He said "I'd go and wake them,
> if — — —"
>
> . . .
>
> And when I found the door was shut,
> I tried to turn the handle, but — — —

Alice's comment shortly after hearing the poem, as she leaves Humpty Dumpty, is "of all the unsatisfactory people I *ever* met — — — — —." Because of forces working against closure in the poem, her comment would seem to be a reprise of the unfinished sentences in the above stanzas.

Now it is not that there are no forces working to close the poem. The line that Alice speaks and that could continue the poem is not spoken immediately after Humpty Dumpty's recitation, nor is it spoken by the character reciting the poem, nor is it a complete couplet, nor is it metrically consistent with the poem. Then, too, we may resolve some of the poem's lack of closure by declaring it humorous, labeling its dissonance and making it acceptable, so that we need not continue to seek closure. Yet the forces working against closure are stronger.

In the first place, the verse purports to tell a narrative, but its story is truncated. The narrator tells of the need to wake the little fishes and of going to the locked door and trying to get through. We expect some kind of resolution: perhaps the narrator breaks through the door, perhaps the door proves sentient and assaults the narrator, perhaps the narrator wastes away to a hummingbird egg as he continually pounds and kicks and knocks. Yet the action is not resolved but interrupted. Similarly, we expect resolution of other hints in the plot: what nefarious deed, requiring the presence of the fishes, does the narrator intend to perpetrate with his kettle of water?

Instead of resolving the plot the poem simply stops, defying closure. And Alice, puzzled, acts out the reader's discomfort over the poem's abrupt completion.

Alice is particularly puzzled by the concluding stanza, the one in which the narrator tries to turn the handle of the door: she pauses, she asks if the poem is over, she finds Humpty Dumpty's dismissal—of the poem and of her—rather sudden. Humpty Dumpty's abrupt good-bye at the end of the poem reinforces the abrupt stopping of the poem itself.

Not only is the narrative action truncated but so too is the sentence begun in the final stanza, as in the other stanzas quoted above. In both the overall plot and also the sentence, the meaning is left hanging: both are semantically incomplete. And the sentence is syntactically incomplete as well.

I can elucidate the syntactic and semantic open-endedness of this verse by comparing it to a rather different open-endedness in verse from *Wonderland*. The verse about the Owl and the Panther concludes thus (in some versions of the poem):

> When the pie was all finished, the Owl, as a boon,
> Was kindly permitted to pocket the spoon:
> While the Panther received knife and fork with a growl,
> And concluded the banquet by — — —

The final line is incomplete, but—guided by meter and rhyme, by our knowledge of panthers, by our knowledge that "by" wants here to be followed by a verb ending in "ing"—we can readily complete the line with "eating the Owl." Even the narrative plot of the verse reaches resolution with this ending, thus reinforcing the implicit closure. With our complicity the verse silently reaches syntactic, semantic, and narrative closure. The *Looking-Glass* verse, Humpty Dumpty's open-ended verse, is rather different. The lines are metrically complete, with appropriate end-rhymes, but semantically incomplete. And the narrative plot is incomplete too. Rather like the later riddle poem, "'*First, the fish must be caught*,'" whose riddle is never solved for us, and perhaps a bit like the riddle posed in his own nursery rhyme, Humpty Dumpty's poem reaches no resolution. Although the stanza reaches prosodic closure, thanks to the tidy end rhyme, the meaning stretches beyond the verse form, eluding closure, eluding the tidy solipsizing of the verse.

Much of the humor of Humpty Dumpty's verse derives from its integration with the narrative, its interruptions, its incompleteness. Some critics find this the least satisfactory of Carroll's verse, and while it is certainly not the best it does become better if we look at it not in isolation but in context. At times the proper unit of analysis is not the poem by itself but the entire dialogue, of which the poem is just part.

Like Humpty Dumpty's poem, if not always to the same degree, the *Looking-Glass* poems are surprisingly integrated into the story, thematically and even physically. Of course, they remain typographically distinct from the prose as well—and again there is a tension between opening and closing. Another site for this tension is the overall structure of *Looking-Glass*. In fact, the greater merging of poetry and prose, compared to *Wonderland*, may in part compensate for a more rigid, closed structure in *Looking-Glass*. Where *Wonderland* describes a relatively aimless wandering, *Looking-Glass* describes a prescribed progression toward a goal, as Alice moves across the chessboard. The individual chapters reinforce the structure by corresponding to individual squares. Carroll counteracts the rigidity of this structure in several ways. One is his placement of lines of asterisks: in *Wonderland* these asterisks, signalling Alice's changes in size, can appear at the end of a chapter, coinciding with and reinforcing a narrative boundary; in *Looking-Glass*, though, Carroll seems careful not to place asterisks, here signalling movement to the next square, at the end of a chapter. Thus Carroll dissipates, a little, the clear demarcations of his narrative. Similarly, in *Looking-Glass* Carroll sometimes does not complete a sentence begun in one chapter until the following chapter: again, Carroll is ameliorating the strict division into chapters. It is as if he wanted to attenuate the rigid boundaries imposed by the chessboard structure. The greater integration of the verse may be similarly compensatory. It attenuates the rigidities of the external scaffolding of the book, much as narrative plays against and dissipates the external scaffolding of the Ulysses story in *Ulysses*.

In fact, Carroll's integration of verse and narrative in *Looking-Glass* is one of the many ways in which he anticipates twentieth-century literature. In some ways *Wonderland* seems rather modern—as in its associative, non-sequential plotting—and in some ways *Looking-Glass* anticipates current fiction. One such way is the way Carroll incorporates verse. His *Looking-Glass* parodies are not true parodies but rather they play against the scaffolding of pre-existing poems, like some of Yeats's poetry, which uses materials in his *A Vision*, yet the images in, say, the Byzantium poems do not need to be followed back to their source before we can appreciate them. Carroll's parodies too can stand alone, divorced from their sources. Though not from the narrative. For the relationship between verse and narrative also seems modern. Recent writers like Vladimir Nabokov, Thomas Pynchon, and Robert Coover have incorporated verse in their novels yet subverted strict boundaries. In Nabokov's *Pale Fire*, for instance, the novel's plot grows out of footnotes presumably annotating a poem: the poem is far from a mere set piece that a character happens to recite. These novelists carry further certain hints in Carroll's work, going farther than he in merging verse and narrative, fiction and reality.

The interaction of poem and narrative in *Looking-Glass* may thus be approaching twentieth-century forms of interpenetration. And Carroll's humor derives in part from this integration and in part from the opposing tendency toward concrete completeness. Likewise it derives in part from parody and in part from simply playing with "real"-world forms. The humor and nonsense and absurdity depend on a confrontation between opposites, a confrontation that we cannot quite resolve in "real"-world terms. Defining "glory" as "a nice knock-down argument" disagrees with our usual use of the term. It is hard even to make it agree metaphorically, as we can when glory is described as clouds that we trail as we come from God. Instead, the odd juxtaposition, the unresolved confrontation, makes us laugh, strikes us as absurd. And we resolve the disparity, a little, by calling it nonsense, something that need not overturn our comfortable real world. Yet despite its resolution it still hints at revolution, still hints at a more serious questioning of reality.

JOHN HOLLANDER

Carroll's Quest Romance

A good deal of nonsense has been written about what Carroll designated, using the word in a rather different sense, his "nonsense" verse. (I have in mind a
range of views, from those that accept at face value whimsy's claims for its own
inherent frivolity, and topical assaults on the puzzles of referentiality [to which
Dodgson's contemporaries contributed] to recently fashionable positions, for example, Michael Holquist ["What Is a Boojum? Nonsense and Modernism,"
reprinted in the Norton Critical Edition of *Alice in Wonderland*, ed. Donald J.
Gray; hereafter called "Gray"]. Since it seems to hold that the arbitrariness of
linguistic meaning governs even sense, this essay's claims that the Snark is about
nothing would either mean that it could be no less profoundly referential than
any poem, or that the critic was at one with the naive reader of childhood whimsy.
It should be clear that I do not include Professor Sewell's *The Field of Nonsense*
in these objections, although remaining unhappy with its rhetorical scope.)
"The game of nonsense," as Elizabeth Sewell called it, is played, in *The Hunting of the Snark*, for very high stakes, even if the frame of the game insists that it
is only penny-ante. It is not only a matter of quips and quibbles stuttered out
frantically at the edge of the abyss, for the kind of criticism of Carroll loosely
called Freudian is of limited value. But in that regard, one thing is certain: the
major writers of the nineteenth century who wrote for the Muse of Childhood
(Andersen, Carroll, Lear) all shared some sexual anomaly, a powerful apparatus
of verbal repression and, more importantly, a *poesis* that allowed the return of
the repressed to blossom in wit and phantasmagoria.

It is hard to think of a writer so obsessed with the purity of discourse — with harder to find a better example — outside of actual dream-work itself — of a text that so energetically discloses what the primary discourse of daily life struggles so to conceal. But we tend to forget that the originality of *The Interpretation of Dreams* lay not so much in its consequences for literary interpretation — the enabling of criticism to treat poems as if they were as personal, private, and obsessively coded as dreams — but in its discovery that dreams were as powerfully and obsessively organized, and as serious in their *mimesis*, as poems. The literary form of modern dreaming is romance, I think, rather than lyric or dramatic. The medieval convention of the dream-vision, perhaps obliquely related to the narrative text in some book that the dreamer has abandoned, in falling asleep, for more weighty and original matter, gives way in poetic history to the intricately allusive, spatially oriented, transumptive structure of Renaissance romantic fable. But it is *The Faerie Queene* which is more dream-like, in this tougher, Freudian sense of being over-determined, than dream-vision.

William Empson correctly observed (in his sage and serious "The Child as Swain" in Gray) that *Alice in Wonderland* was more of a dream-vision (with its concentration on the dreamer, her falls and changes of size, and the kinds of situation she encounters, at which the way in which she is behaving is usually at issue) than *Through the Looking-Glass*. (On the related issues of pastoral and romance, we may not actually differ: in English, Sidney and Spenser taught the second of these modes to contain the first.) The latter has more the form of a romance, which relates it to *The Hunting of the Snark* (aside from the question of Carroll's association of that poem with "Jabberwocky," of which more later). This is not only because it has a quest story (ephebe-pawn to move through chessboard squares to be queened), nor because its episodes are mapped by its scheme, while its actual regions and places are more allusively allegorical than most of those in *Alice in Wonderland*, etc. *Through the Looking-Glass* also has an allusive relation to the earlier book. For example, Hatta and Haigha, the "Anglo-Saxon messengers" in chapter 7, are metamorphoses of the Mad Hatter and the March Hare (Tenniel's illustrations confirm this), although the narrative points only toward such associations as with Hengist and Horsa, say (and perhaps, as Harry Morgan Ayres suggested, with an Anglo-Saxon scholar named Haigh). The multiple allusiveness of the names and attributes of the characters in the second book is typical of both dreams and major romances like *The Faerie Queene*.

Similarly, the ways in which parody is employed in the two books are significant. In the first one, Alice continually finds herself subverting the education routines she is called upon by the adult creatures to perform. In the course of speaking a piece, she finds herself unwittingly parodying it, and the pieties of Isaac Watts come out full of nastiness, guile and what Delmore Schwartz called "the scrimmage of appetite everywhere." (In the parody of "The Sluggard," the suppression, by reason of the Mock Turtle's interruption, of the final words — "But the panther received knife and fork with a growl, / And concluded the banquet by — " [inevitably — "eating the owl"] was clearly designed to be noticed by the amused children reading it.) But the inset verse in *Through the Looking-Glass* is generally more complex in its nature and in the role it plays in the narrative. Alice hears these poems and songs, rather than helplessly producing them, and the first of these, "Jabberwocky," remains a central subtext. The parodies here are of romantic poetry (Hood, Moore, Scott, and, of course, Wordsworth), the parodic modes ranging from univocal pastiche to revisionary satire so subtle and deep as to approach true poetry on its own, in a mode of the ridiculous sublime. Thus, in the White Knight's song (so framed by titles and meta-titles that we should simply call it that), the remarkable conclusion goes beyond the mere parody of "Resolution and Independence" of its earlier published version. As the song of the absent-minded, poetical White Knight, whose access to the truth about his own originality is characteristically blocked (the tune of the song is *not* his "own invention," as Alice observes), its conclusion does a great turn on Wordsworthian involuntary memory generally:

> And now if e'er by chance I put
>   My fingers into glue,
> Or madly squeeze a right-hand foot
>   Into a left-hand shoe,
> Or if I drop upon my toe
>   A very heavy weight,
> I weep, for it reminds me so
> Of that old man I used to know —

(the "for" in "I weep, *for* it reminds me so" is brilliant here, in that the joke about present and absent feeling aside, it does indeed lead to a catalogue of recollections, totally absent from the 1856 version of the parody reprinted in Gray) —

> Whose look was mild, whose speech was slow,
> Whose hair was whiter than the snow,
> Whose face was very like a crow,
> With eyes, like cinders, all aglow,
> Who seemed distracted with his woe,
> Who rocked his body to and fro,
> And muttered mumblingly and low,

As if his mouth were full of dough,
Who snorted like a buffalo —
That summer evening, long ago,
A-sitting on a gate.

The White Knight seems never less ridiculous than when, in bidding Alice farewell on her last crossing into the square of the end of her quest and hearing that she has liked the song, replies "I hope so" (doubtfully), and "but you didn't cry so much as I thought you would." Just as it requires the larger genre of comedy to contain within its world a satirist, so it requires the realm of romance to contain within it a poet.

Alice in Wonderland does indeed occasionally move into the allusive mode of romance, for example in the scene in chapter 8 in which Alice, finally reaching her longed-for garden, finds it full of English history. The gardeners painting the white roses red are enacting a child's confusion about Yorkist and Lancastrian roses succeeding each other; the gardeners seem to have wandered in from *Richard II* (act 3, scene 4); and the Queen of Hearts, whose garden it is, eventually appears as a sort of Bloody Mary, ordering beheadings left and right. In *Through the Looking-Glass*, the transformed topoi are more evocatively shadowed. The wandering wood or forest of Error in *The Faerie Queene* (act 1, scene 1) is the place where a lady and a lion roam, and where you can lose your moral way. Its avatar is the wood behind Ludlow Castle, in Shropshire, as it is figured in the dangerous forest in *Comus*, through which another virginal Alice (Alice Egerton, masquing The Lady) must be safely conducted. The wood where everything and every person loses its name is a strangely redeemed version of these forests, in that because of its dislocations and crises of identity, what may be a unique event in the two *Alice* books is enabled. Physical contact between Alice and the other personages and creatures is usually unpleasant or at least inconvenient. But as Alice moves through the wood with the Fawn she has encountered there, and who has forgotten its nature along with its name, a familiar emblem (Lady with Lion — Lady with Unicorn) takes on another aspect: "So they walked on together through the wood, Alice with her arms clasped lovingly around the soft neck of the Fawn, till they came out into another open field, and here the Fawn gave a sudden bound into the air, and shook itself free from Alice's arm." In a sudden burst of returning knowledge, Alice loses her "dear little fellow-traveller," and the sole moment of affectionate and gratifying touching in her two fictional worlds (aside from the contact between girl and kitten in the outer frame of the looking-glass realm) comes to an end. In the episode preceding her arrival in the forest of anonymy, the gentleman sitting opposite Alice in the railway-carriage is dressed in white paper, which is certainly an allusion to official parliamentary documents (and thus may have provided the cue for Tenniel's caricature of Disraeli in his illustration of the scene). This scene partakes of the bungled history lesson in the Queen of Hearts' garden, but the episode of the wood feels far more like high-romantic fable.

The looking-glass world is generally more mythopoetically active than what is down the rabbit-hole. In *Alice in Wonderland* creatures from phrase and fable, sometimes with topical allusiveness to the court of Dodgsonian girls, share epistemological status with natural ones; and save for the baby who becomes a pig (having had its animal nature totally elicited by too much rubifacient and erotic pepper), it is Alice who metamorphoses, at least in size, and thereby in condition. The one exemplary instance of the generation of what a modern nominalist like W.V. Quine (who once remarked that he didn't want anything more in his philosophy than there were in heaven and earth) would call a "queer entity" is itself almost didactic, and occurs in a scene of instruction. The Gryphon in chapter 9 is a creature of classical mythology and medieval heraldry, and his companion, the Mock Turtle, is created not by the poetic magic of "nonsense" or of allusive revision, not puns or anagrams, but by an otherwise fruitless algebraic mistake. The elementary error of misplacing parentheses is demonstrated as if in some invalid enthymeme: There is mock-turtle soup; therefore there are mock-turtles (from which the soup is presumably made). But the error is one of confusing what is, logically, "mock (turtle soup)" — which is what the name means — with "(mock-turtle) soup." [This lesson is taught again in *Sylvie and Bruno Concluded*, when Bruno, counting pigs in a field, announces that there are "about a thousand and four"; when instructed in the notion of rounding-out he protests that there are about a thousand spread over the field, and four "here by the window," and that it was only the four that he could be "sure about." Again, misplaced parentheses: (about a thousand) and (four) vs. (about) (a thousand and four).] Perhaps the most profound antithetical joke about the education of Victorian girlhood made in the Mock-Turtle's account of his schooling under the sea is the apparently trivial one about the Gryphon's (not, appropriately, the Mock Turtle's) Classical master, "an old crab," who taught "Laughing and Grief." The joke is not merely the superficial pun on "Latin and Greek," nor the more interesting allusion to Comedy and Tragedy, but instead lies in the matter of expressions of emotion being "taught" or conventionalized. One can imagine Dodgson's great ambivalence with respect to this: it is at once anti-Darwinian in one sense, and a triumph of nurture over nature, and at the same time sounds a menacing note to the effect that the giggles and tears of the beloved Muse-children might have been acquired contrivances — an almost Blakean notion.

But in the second book, the mythopoetic imagination is always more deeply at work. There is the matter of memory and secondariness which I touched on earlier: *Through the Looking-Glass* in fact remembers and transforms elements in the first book (the middle-class Gryphon and Mock Turtle, beside the sea, are replaced by the working-class Carpenter and Walrus by the sea-side in Tweedle-dee's ballad, for example). Chess has provided an allegorical milieu since the Middle Ages, and the child as pawn in the adult world of strategy, progressing by direct degrees to an adult role herself, is a more complex romance protagonist than a dreamer shuffled among cards. And finally, the matter of language itself is constantly foregrounded in the looking-glass world, with much more being made of the relation of names to things, and, even more central, in the theory of the "portmanteau word" in Humpty Dumpty's scholia on "Jabberwocky," which applies to the whole history of modern romance, from the nature of naming in *The Faerie Queene* to the very fabric of *Finnegans Wake*, not to speak of the hieroglyphic language of half-concealing, half-disclosing Freudian dream-work.

And yet we tend to forget, I think, that Humpty Dumpty's explication of the miniature quest-romance of "Jabberwocky," bringing reason to rhyme as it does, represents nonetheless one of the many sorts of deflection or evasion with which Carroll frames so much of his "nonsense" verse. When she first deciphers the mirror-writing of the text of the ballad in the first chapter, Alice observes that "it seems very pretty . . . but it's *rather* hard to understand." This might apply to much poetry. But she concludes, "however, *somebody* killed *something*: that's clear, at any rate —." Yes, somebody killed something, and this is precisely what Humpty Dumpty, in his pursuit of etymological glosses, neglects to observe. "Jabberwocky" is a great heroic tale, and the son, the "he" of the poem, is one with the tribe of Cadmus and Beowulf and Siegfried and Red-crosse, and his song of sallying forth, preparatory meditation, conquest, and triumphal return is framed in the identical stanza of prologue and epilogue, a cluster of stage-setting details which Humpty Dumpty (who "can explain all the poems that ever were invented — and a good many that haven't been invented just yet" — he is some kind of generative grammarian) so memorably annotates. But Alice's initial response remains absolutely central, and Humpty Dumpty's philology averts its gaze from what she knows.

Carroll's other quest romances in verse, such as the Pig-Tale in *Sylvie and Bruno*, likewise seek to deflect attention from their mode of conditional heroism, but in different ways. The pig who "made his moan . . . Because he could not jump" sits alone "Beside a ruined Pump" in a scene of picturesque melancholy (even "made his moan" is a Spenserian-Keatsian locution); he comes to grief when he mistakes the advice of a frog in the matter of athletic training, till "Uprose that pig and rushed, full whack, / Against the ruined Pump" (the stanza's last line adds: "It was a fatal jump!"). But there is no moral, and he is memorialized only by the frog (sitting "on the ruined Pump"), silent, because with the death of the pig, he would get no fee for his jumping-lessons. But the refrain-like "ruined Pump," like the "A-sitting on a gate" of the White Knight's song, has the last, echoing word.

It was nominally Humpty Dumpty's theory of the portmanteau word, and the linguistic allusions to "Jabberwocky," that caused Carroll to say in the preface to *The Hunting of the Snark* that it was "to some extent connected with the lay of the Jabberwock." I should, however, prefer to observe with Alice that, in the case of the bedevilled Argonauts of the *Snark, some people* went after *something:* that's clear at any rate. The realms of "nonsense" verse and child's dream world are alike for Carroll in legitimating high romance, and the non-sense-verse elements in the unfolding of the quest of the Snark are a necessary part of its *poesis*. Nonsense verse deflects attention from its sense by pretending to be silly, even though the maker of it may be as sincere in this pretense as the dreamer is in an intention to sleep on undisturbed by anything meaningful. The method in the madness need not call for an uncovering of repressed material alone. In *Sylvie and Bruno*, the mad gardener's song which runs throughout is sometimes keyed to the narrative in a variety of ways (passing figures in a stanza of the song—like the Elephant that practised on a fife—are actualized in the story, for example). But the paradigmatic structure of the stanzas—"He thought he saw X; He looked again and saw it was Y; 'Z', he said " —suggests that "Z" is a response only to Y. But often it applies to both. Thus:

> He thought he saw a Rattlesnake
> That questioned him in Greek:
> He looked again, and saw it was
> The Middle of Next Week.
> "The one thing I regret," he said
> "Is that it cannot speak!"

A Hermetic serpent asking sphinx-like questions about the future metamor-phoses into a prophesiable future, but the serpent is no oracle. What is regret-table is that The Middle of Next Week cannot speak now (only, as it were, *then*) and that the Rattlesnake will not speak answers, at any rate, which amounts to much the same thing. Even frightening portents seldom deliver true prophecy, save by the most twisted and figurative of readings.

Behind the nonsense of *The Hunting of the Snark*, then, lies its serious quest story. W. H. Auden, both in *The Enchafèd Flood* and in a series of lec-tures on The Quest in literature, included the voyages of both the Snark-hunters and Edward Lear's *The Jumblies* among the company of *Moby-Dick* and "The Narrative of A. Gordon Pym," and by calling attention to its generality he did something useful in combatting misplaced literalisms among interpreters. Of the history of detailed readings of the poem, I should say that F. C. S. Schiller's celebrated parodic commentary of 1901 (originally in a parody issue of *Mind* and reprinted in its entirety in Martin Gardner's *The Annotated Snark*) remains the best, not because the Snark is read jokingly as a Hegelian Absolute which at least outjokes whimsy into something nearer the truth than "nonsense," but because some of its mock-glosses of particular stanzas are better and more memorable than solemn ones might be. Just as some sort of Borgesian fiction about, say, a Shakespearean crux may ring truer than a serious, half-reasonably grounded scholarly "suggestion," so (of a resonant stanza—fit 4, st. 5):

> I said it in Hebrew—I said it in Dutch—
>   I said it in German and Greek;
> But I wholly forgot (and it vexes me much)
>   That English is what you speak!

"The accounts of the Absolute in German and Greek are famous, while the Hebrew and Dutch probably both refer to Spinoza, who was a Dutch Jew, although he wrote in bad Latin. The forgetting to speak (and write) English is a common symptom of the Absolute." Leaving aside the matter of these being the Baker's lines to the Bellman, and the "it" being his metaphysical vulnerability to Boojums, totally transcended (*aufgehoben*), Schiller's gloss nonetheless, like those of Humpty Dumpty or of Bentley on Milton, points to a real question of why just *those* languages, and not the more usual French or Latin, for example. And in general, thinking in fact of the Snark as a Black Hole of mystification, some Greco-German Absolute, will let one do better with the rest of the poem than most suggestions will.

But if one is to read cues as clues, the canonical one, repeated six times, is certainly there. Once it has been introduced by the Baker's uncle, and reiterated by the Bellman, the famous stanza heads all of the last four fits:

> They sought it with thimbles, they sought it with care;
>   They pursued it with forks and hope;
> They threatened its life with a railway-share;
>   They charmed it with smiles and soap.

I suppose I should say right off that the "it" of these lines is probably something less than the Absolute, but which has been magnified by neurotic terror into something that, for the quest story, will do as well. Female sexuality—a distorted version of *das Ewig-Weibliche*, the "eternal feminine" of *Faust* for a spirit that remained blocked by the sexuality—seems to be the point here. (This was the view of W. H. Auden, advanced in conversation about twenty years ago, and without reference to or discussion of the relevant passages.) Thimbles, care (the effect of the whimsical zeugma here and in the next line is only momentarily to deflect attention away from the concrete entities of care and hope employed in the hunt); forks, hope: the domestic objects and the inner states marshalled in a kind of courtship. The world of the broker is alien and intrusive in that of the Victorian *gynacaeum*. The smiles and soap make amends for this. The fear of the less-than-erotically-secure of being "softly and suddenly" swallowed up in an abyss of feminity is materialized in the last glimpse of the unnameable Baker:

> They beheld him — their Baker — their hero unnamed
>   On the top of a neighboring crag,
>
> Erect and sublime, for one moment of time.
>   In the next, that wild figure they saw
> (As if stung by a spasm) plunge into a chasm,
>   While they waited and listened in awe.
>
> (fit 8, sts. 4–5)

The name of the Snark — Carroll himself suggested the portmanteau snail + shark — is full of suggestions of snarling and snagging, as in the stanza commencing with the magnificent line (consider the final word)

> Then the bowsprit got mixed with the rudder sometimes
>   A thing, as the Bellman remarked,
> That frequently happens in tropical climes,
>   When a vessel is, so to speak, "snarked."
>
> (fit 2, st. 7)

— but here the sense is of a vessel spooked as well. If the Snark is indeed like a viscous mollusc with teeth in it, however, it is also like a snake in the dark. "Just the place for a Snark" is the voyager's paradise of land where, quite properly for quest-romance, the poem starts in the middle of the journey.

But even the Bellman's instructions in the second fit (stanzas 15–20), and his recitation of the "five unmistakable marks" by which a Snark may be known are significant about femininity. Snarks taste "meagre and hollow, but crisp: / Like a coat that is rather too tight in the waist, / With a flavour of Will-o-the-Wisp." Snarks get up too late, don't get jokes nor tolerate puns, are fond of bathing-machines, and are (and here Dodgson would least like to think about what Carroll is writing) ambitious. And some are Boojums, at which the Baker faints to end the fit. I find it interesting that the third fit immediately thereafter commences with a stanza that heralds the repeated clue-quatrain in its perfect syntactic paradigm:

> They roused him with muffins — they roused him with ice —
> They roused him with mustard and cress —
> They roused him with jam and judicious advice —
> They set him conundrums to guess.

(fit 3, st. 1)

(The alliterative jam and just counsel in the third line seem to come from the "Little birds are feeding / Justices with jam" in the Introductory Verses to the Pig-Tale in *Sylvie and Bruno Concluded*). In any event, twice more (in fits 4 and 5) is the syntactic paradigm repeated, hammering it into consciousness in the poem — if not into truth — by its own "rule of three." The most significant repetitions in the poem are those of the alliterating B's of the ten voyagers, all bachelors, whose chart of the sea is "a perfect and absolute blank" and who are doomed, in pursuing the strange Snark, to encounter in it the more horribly alliteratively *heimlich* Boojum after all. (In the digressive episodes, the Banker is maddened by the Bandersnatch, but the Jubjub bird, also imported from "Jabberwocky," is a highly moral, although desperate and passionate, creature, the contemplation of which leads to a benign scene of instruction and a consequent friendship between Butcher and Beaver.)

But it is ultimately the Bellman and the Baker who matter most. The former, having none of the "drowzy charm" of Milton's Bellman in *Il Penseroso* (Carroll quotes from that poem in his preface) is one of the poet's surrogates in the poem; the Baker, with his forgotten name and abandoned forty-two parcels (the years of Dodgson's life — I am sure that a scholarly conjecture is right in this), is more clearly the major one (see *The Annotated Snark*). With such a central protagonist vanished, there is nothing more of the poem to be said. Carroll's continued insistence that the whole poem started with the *vers donné* of the last line — "For the Snark was a Boojum, you see" — may be a little like Poe's account of the composition of "The Raven" in what it directs attention away from. Certainly the Baker's fear is as much of a driving force in the poem's workings as the Bellman's questing, but neither Captain Ahab nor Coleridge's Mariner seem pertinent here, insofar as character and motivation are concerned. And yet, in the end, the Hunting of the Snark, the quest itself, is seen to have had the power of character and motive that even its central characters do not. And it remains one of the major quests of our romantic literature, having become part of our conceptual landscape. Whether we think of Spenser's Guyon, believing he knows what the Bower of Bliss really is as he sets out to destroy it, or of a sleuth in any modern detective-story, every Snark — and here I should rather put the question of engulfment aside, and return to the joked-about Absolute — will always turn out to have been a sort of Boojum. The line that came into Carroll's head, and which required the whole verse romance to give it meaning, ends up by having become true, true of all of our stories and of, alas, all of our lives. Which is what real nonsense is for.

Chronology

1832   Charles Lutwidge Dodgson born on January 27 in Daresbury, Cheshire, to the Reverend Charles Dodgson and Frances Jane Lutwidge Dodgson. He is the third child and eldest son of their eleven children (seven daughters, four sons).

1832–43 Dodgson educated at home: found to be left-handed and afflicted with a stammer (as are most of his siblings).

1843   The family moves to Croft, in Yorkshire, where the Reverend Charles Dodgson has been made Rector.

1844–46 Dodgson attends Richmond Grammar School in Yorkshire. Entertains family with poems, drawings, and games.

1846–50 Dodgson attends Rugby College; although he does well there, he is not happy in the public school atmosphere.

1850   Dodgson at home, working on family magazines such as *The Rectory Umbrella* and *Useful and Instructive Poetry*.

1851–54 Attends Christ Church College, Oxford. Enters as a Commoner two days before his mother dies (on January 24). Contributes to the *Oxonian Advertiser* and the *Whitby Gazette*. In 1852, awarded a Studentship which will provide him with an income for the rest of his life. (The Studentship stipulates that he remain celibate and take Holy Orders.) In 1854, becomes Bachelor of Arts, with a First Class degree in Mathematics.

1855   Made Sub-Librarian and Master of the House at Christ Church; becomes Mathematical Lecturer. Writes *Mischmasch*, a scrapbook which contains, among other writings, the first stanza of "Jabberwocky," listed as "Stanza of Anglo-Saxon Poetry."

1856   Publishes a number of parodies, including "Upon a Lonely Moor"
        ("Resolution and Independence"), under the name Lewis Carroll,
        derived from Latinate forms of Charles and Lutwidge. (The argument
        that he may have been influenced in choosing his alias by the names of
        two of his sisters, Caroline and Louisa, is unverified.) Buys his first
        camera; beginning his lifelong devotion to photography. Meets the
        daughters of the Dean of Christ Church, among them, Alice Pleasance
        Liddell, who will become Alice in Wonderland.

1857   Dodgson takes his M.A. Befriends and photographs various Pre-
        Raphaelite poets and painters, as well as Thackeray and Tennyson.

1860   First mathematical publications, *A Syllabus of Plane Algebraical
        Geometry* and *Notes on the First Two Books of Euclid, Designed for
        Candidates for Responsions*, both intended as aids for students.

1861   Dodgson decides not to take full Holy Orders as the Studentship stip-
        ulated, in part because he is an ardent theatergoer. Dean Liddell
        allows him to be ordained as Deacon instead. In this capacity, he occa-
        sionally baptizes infants and officiates at funerals. Begins his Register
        of Correspondence, an account, with a summary, of every letter he
        writes or receives: at his death, it numbers 98,721 pieces of mail.

1862   Deacon Dodgson, Canon Duckworth, and the three Liddell sisters take
        a boat ride up the river to Godstow on July 4. On that trip, Dodgson
        amuses the children with the story of Alice's adventures under ground.
        Alice Liddell begs him to write down the account. He begins work on
        what is to be *Alice's Adventures under Ground*.

1863   Publishes *Enunciations of Euclid*.

1864   Dodgson completes a special, hand-illustrated version of *Alice's Ad-
        ventures under Ground* as a present for Alice Liddell. In the mean-
        while, at the urging of George MacDonald's children, he has begun a
        revision of the book for publication, to be illustrated by John Tenniel.
        He sends Tenniel a photograph of another child-friend, Mary Hilton
        Badcock, from which to do the illustrations. Publishes *A Guide to the
        Mathematical Student in Reading, Reviewing, and Working Examples*.

1865   First publication of *Alice's Adventures in Wonderland* in July; Dodgson
        unhappy with the printing. Withdraws the book (sending the poor
        copies to America) and has it reprinted and published in November.

Generally well reviewed, the book sells quite well after a slow start. Publishes the satires "The New Method of Evaluation as Applied to π" and " The Dynamics of a Parti-cle."

1866   Second American edition of *Alice's Adventures in Wonderland*. Dodgson publishes *Condensation of Determinants*.

1867   Publishes *An Elementary Treatise on Determinants*. Publishes "Bruno's Revenge" in a children's magazine; the story is the basis for the *Sylvie and Bruno* books. Takes a tour of Russia.

1868   Dodgson's father dies on June 21—"the greatest blow that has ever fallen on my life." Dodgson publishes *The Fifth Book of Euclid Treated Algebraically* and the satire "The Offer of the Clarendon Trustees." A conversation with child-friend Alice Raikes gives Dodgson idea for *Through the Looking-Glass*.

1869   Publishes collection of verse, *Phantasmagoria*.

1871   *Through the Looking-Glass and What Alice Found There*, with illustrations by John Tenniel, published in December. Immediately successful.

1872   Publishes satire "The New Belfry of Christ Church, Oxford."

1873   Publishes satire "The Vision of the Three T's."

1874   Publishes book for students, *Examples in Arithmetic*, and satire, "The Blank Cheque."

1875   Publishes polemic "Some Popular Fallacies about Vivisection."

1876   Publishes *The Hunting of the Snark: An Agony in Eight Fits*, with illustrations by Henry Holiday (except for a picture of the Snark, which Dodgson deletes). It is dedicated to child-friend Gertrude Chataway. Refuses to have his caricature done for *Vanity Fair* by Leslie Ward, as "nothing would be more unpleasant for me than to have my face known to strangers." Also returns all mail addressed to Lewis Carroll.

1879   Publishes *Euclid and His Modern Rivals*.

1881   Dodgson resigns his Lectureship at Oxford, although he continues to live at Christ Church, hoping to devote more time to his writing.

1882   Elected Curator of the Senior Common Room at Christ Church.

1883   Publishes *Rhyme? and Reason?*, a collection of verse, containing new material and previously published poems.

1885   Publishes *A Tangled Tale*, a series of previously published mathematical problems posed as short stories.

1886   Teaches logic in several girls' schools in Oxford. Facsimile edition published of *Alice's Adventures under Ground*. Stage version of *Alice in Wonderland* produced, created by H. Savile Clark.

1887   Publishes *The Game of Logic*, a serious and nonsensical introduction to logic.

1888   Publishes *Curiosa Mathematica, Part I: A New Theory of Parallels*.

1889   Publishes *Sylvie and Bruno*, a highly moral fairy tale, and *The Nursery Alice*, a picture book of *Alice* for the very young.

1893   Publishes *Sylvie and Bruno Concluded* and *Curiosa Mathematica, Part II: Pillow Problems Thought Out During Sleepless Nights*.

1896   Publishes *Symbolic Logic*.

1898   Dies of a bronchial infection at his sisters' home, "The Chestnuts," in Guildford on January 14.

1928   Alice Liddell Hargreaves auctions her handwritten manuscript of *Alice's Adventures under Ground* for £15,400 — the highest price ever bid for a book in a British auction and more than the buyer had just paid for a Shakespeare first folio.

1932   Alice Liddell Hargreaves is awarded an honorary degree from Columbia University for being Alice.

1934   Alice Liddell Hargreaves dies at her home in Westerham, Kent, on November 16.

Contributors

HAROLD BLOOM, Sterling Professor of the Humanities at Yale University, is the author of *The Anxiety of Influence, Poetry and Repression*, and many other volumes of literary criticism. His forthcoming study, *Freud: Transference and Authority*, attempts a full-scale reading of all of Freud's major writings. A MacArthur Prize Fellow, he is general editor of five series of literary criticism published by Chelsea House.

ROBERT MARTIN ADAMS is the author of *Nil, After Joyce*, and *The Roman Stamp*.

JAN B. GORDON is Professor of English at Doshisha University in Kyoto, Japan. He has published many articles on the poetry and criticism of the last century.

NINA AUERBACH is Associate Professor of English at the University of Pennsylvania. She is the author of *Communities of Women: An Idea in Fiction* and *Woman and the Demon: The Life of a Victorian Myth*.

PETER HEATH is Professor of Philosophy at the University of Virginia. His books include *The Philosopher's Alice*.

EDMUND MILLER is a freelance critic and poet, and the author of *The Nadine Poems*.

ALWIN L. BAUM teaches literature at the State University of New York at Buffalo.

JUDITH CREWS is Lecturer in English and Comparative Literature at the American College in Paris.

EDWARD GUILIANO is Professor of English at the New York Institute of Technology. He is the editor of *Lewis Carroll Observed, Lewis Carroll: A Cele-*

bration, The Wasp in a Wig: A Suppressed Episode of Through the Looking-Glass, and *The Complete Illustrated Works of Lewis Carroll.*

DONALD RACKIN is Professor of English at Temple University. He has written extensively on Lewis Carroll and is the editor of *Academe.*

BEVERLY LYON CLARK is Assistant Professor of English at Wheaton College. She is the author of *Reflections of Fantasy: The Mirror-Worlds of Carroll, Nabokov, and Pynchon.*

JOHN HOLLANDER, the distinguished poet, is A. Bartlett Giamatti Professor of English at Yale University. His most recent books include *The Figure of Echo* and *Powers of Thirteen*, a poetic sequence.

Bibliography

Alexander, Peter. "Logic and the Humor of Lewis Carroll." *Proceedings of the Leeds Philosophical and Literary Society* 6 (1951): 551–66.

Arnoldi, Richard. "Parallels Between *Our Mutual Friend* and the Alice Books." *Children's Literature* 1 (1972): 54–57.

Auden, W. H. *The Enchafèd Flood: or The Romantic Iconography of the Sea.* London: Faber & Faber, 1951.

———. "Lewis Carroll." In *Forewords and Afterwords by W. H. Auden*, selected by Edward Mendelson, 283–93. New York: Random House, 1973.

Avery, Gillian. *Nineteenth Century Children: Heroes and Heroines in English Children's Stories 1780–1900.* London: Hodder & Stoughton, 1965.

Blake, Kathleen. *Play, Games, and Sport: The Literary Works of Lewis Carroll.* Ithaca, N.Y.: Cornell University Press, 1974.

Bloch, Robert. "All in a Golden Afternoon." *Fantasy & Science Fiction* 10, no. 6 (1956): 105–26.

Bowman, Isa. *The Story of Lewis Carroll.* London: J. M. Dent, 1899.

Brockway, Robert W. "The *Descensus ad Inferos* of Lewis Carroll." *Dalhousie Review* 62, no. 1 (1982): 36–43.

Brown, Fredric. *Night of the Jabberwock.* New York: Quill, 1984.

Cammaerts, Emile. *The Poetry of Nonsense.* New York: Dutton, 1926. Reprint. Darby, Pa.: Folcroft Library Editions, 1971.

Cixous, Hélène. "Introduction to Lewis Carroll's *Through the Looking Glass* and *The Hunting of the Snark*," translated by Marie Maclean. *New Literary History* 13, no. 2 (1982): 231–51.

Clark, Anne, *Lewis Carroll: A Biography.* New York: Schocken, 1979.

Cohen, Morton. *Lewis Carroll and Alice 1832–1982.* New York: Pierpont Morgan Library, 1982.

———. "Lewis Carroll and Victorian Morality." In *Sexuality and Victorian Literature*, edited by Don Richard Cox, 3–19. Knoxville: University of Tennessee Press, 1984.

Cohen, Morton N., and Roger Lancelyn Green, eds. *The Selected Letters of Lewis Carroll.* New York: Pantheon, 1982.

Collingwood, Stuart Dodgson. *The Life and Letters of Lewis Carroll.* London: T. Fisher Unwin, 1898.

Cook, Albert. *The Dark Voyage and the Golden Mean: A Philosophy of Comedy*. Cambridge: Harvard University Press, 1949.

Coveney, Peter. *The Image of Childhood: The Individual and Society: A Study of the Theme in English Literature*. 1957. Rev. ed. Baltimore: Penguin, 1967.

Cripps, Elizabeth A. "*Alice* and the Reviewers." *Children's Literature* 11 (1983): 32–48.

Crofte-Cooke, Rupert. *Feasting with Panthers: A New Consideration of Some Late Victorian Writers*. New York: Holt, Rinehart & Winston, 1968.

Deleuze, Gilles. "The Schizophrenic and Language: Surface and Depth in Lewis Carroll and Antonin Artaud." Translated by Josué V. Harari. In *Textual Strategies: Perspectives in Post-Structuralist Criticism*, edited by Josué V. Harari, 277–95. Ithaca, N.Y.: Cornell University Press, 1979.

Dierickx, J. "Some Belated Remarks on the Frenchification of Snarks." *Revue des Langues Vivantes* 40 (1974): 466–73.

Dolitsky, Marlene. *Under the Tumtum Tree: From Nonsense to Sense: A Study in Non-automatic Comprehension*. Amsterdam: Benjamins, 1984.

English Language Notes 20, no. 2 (December 1982). Special Lewis Carroll issue.

Ettleson, Abraham. *Lewis Carroll's* Through the Looking-Glass *Decoded*. New York: Philosophical Library, 1966.

Fisher, John, ed. *The Magic of Lewis Carroll*. New York: Simon & Schuster, 1973.

Flescher, Jacqueline. "The Language of Nonsense in *Alice*." *Yale French Studies* 43 (1969): 128–44.

Fraser, Morris. *The Death of Narcissus*. London: Secker & Warburg, 1976.

Gabriele, Mark. "*Alice in Wonderland*: Problem of Identity— Aggressive Content and Form Control." *American Imago* 39, no. 4 (1982): 369–89.

Gardner, Martin, ed. *The Annotated Alice*. 1960. Rev. ed. Harmondsworth, England: Penguin, 1970.

———, ed. *The Annotated Snark*. New York: Simon & Schuster, 1962.

Gernsheim, Helmut. *Lewis Carroll, Photographer*. New York: Chanticleer Press, 1949.

Graham, Neilson. "Sanity, Madness, and Alice." *Ariel* 4, no. 2 (1973): 80–89.

Gray, Donald J., ed. *Lewis Carroll*: Alice in Wonderland. A Norton Critical Edition. New York: Norton, 1971.

Green, Roger Lancelyn. *Lewis Carroll*. London: Bodley Head, 1960.

———, ed. *The Diaries of Lewis Carroll*, 2 vols. New York: Oxford University Press, 1953.

———, ed. *The Lewis Carroll Handbook*. London: Oxford University Press, 1962.

Greenacre, Phyllis. *Swift and Carroll: A Psychoanalytic Study of Two Lives*. New York: International Universities Press, 1955.

Guiliano, Edward. "Lewis Carroll: A Sesquicentennial Guide to Research." *Dickens Studies Annual* 10 (1982): 263–310.

———, ed. *Lewis Carroll: A Celebration: Essays on the Occasion of the 150th Anniversary of the Birth of Charles Lutwidge Dodgson*. New York: Clarkson N. Potter, 1982.

———, ed. *Lewis Carroll Observed: A Collection of Unpublished Photographs, Drawings, Poetry, and New Essays*. New York: Clarkson N. Potter, 1976.

———, ed. *The Wasp in a Wig: A Suppressed Episode of* Through the Looking-Glass, with preface, introduction, and notes by Martin Gardner. New York: Lewis Carroll Society of North America, 1978.

Halpern, Sidney. "The Mother-Killer." *The Psychoanalytic Review* 52, no. 2 (1965): 71–74.

Hancher, Michael. "Humpty Dumpty and Verbal Meaning." *The Journal of Aesthetics and Art Criticism* 40, no. 1 (1981): 49–58.

————. *On the Writing, Illustration and Publication of Lewis Carroll's* Alice Books. London: Macmillan Children's Books, 1984.

Hardy, Barbara. *Tellers and Listeners: The Narrative Imagination.* London: Athlone, 1975.

Hatch, Evelyn M. *A Selection from the Letters of Lewis Carroll to His Child-Friends.* London: Macmillan, 1933.

Helson, Ravenna. "The Psychological Origins of Fantasy for Children in Mid-Victorian England." *Children's Literature* 3 (1974): 66–76.

Henkle, Roger B. *Comedy and Culture: England 1820–1900.* Princeton: Princeton University Press, 1980.

————. "The Mad Hatter's World." *Virginia Quarterly Review* 49, no. 1 (1973): 99–117.

Hennelly, Mark M., Jr. "Alice's Big Sister: Fantasy and the Adolescent." *Journal of Popular Culture* 16, no. 1 (1982): 72–87.

Higbie, Robert. "Lewis Carroll and the Victorian Reaction against Doubt." *Thalia* 3, no. 1 (1980): 21–28.

Hollander, John. "'Haddocks' Eyes': A Note on the Theory of Titles." In *Vision and Resonance: Two Senses of Poetic Form*, 2d ed., 212–27. New Haven: Yale University Press, 1985.

Hudson, Derek. *Lewis Carroll.* London: Constable, 1954.

Huxley, Francis. *The Raven and the Writing Desk.* New York: Harper & Row, 1977.

Inglis, Fred. *The Promise of Happiness: Value and Meaning in Children's Fiction.* Cambridge: Cambridge University Press, 1981.

Jabberwocky: The Journal of the Lewis Carroll Society, 1969–.

Jackson, Rosemary. *Fantasy: The Literature of Subversion.* London: Methuen, 1981.

Jorgens, Jack J. "Alice Our Contemporary." *Children's Literature* 1 (1972): 152–61.

Kelly, Richard. *Lewis Carroll.* Boston: Twayne, 1977.

Kenner, Hugh. "Alice in Chapelizod." In *Dublin's Joyce*, 276–300. London: Chatto & Windus, 1955.

Kibel, Alvin C. "Logic and Satire in *Alice in Wonderland.*" *American Scholar* 43 (1974): 605–29.

Kincaid, James R. "Alice's Invasion of Wonderland." *PMLA* 88 (1973): 92–99.

Kirk, Daniel F. *Charles Dodgson: Semeiotician.* Gainesville: University of Florida Press, 1962.

Koelb, Clayton. *The Incredulous Reader: Literature and the Function of Disbelief.* Ithaca, N.Y.: Cornell University Press, 1984.

Lehmann, John F. *Lewis Carroll and the Spirit of Nonsense.* Nottingham, England: University of Nottingham Press, 1974.

Lennon, Florence Becker. *The Life of Lewis Carroll.* New York: Collier Books, 1962.

————. *Victoria through the Looking-Glass.* New York: Simon & Schuster, 1945.

Madden, William A. "Framing the *Alices.*" *PMLA* 101 (1986): 362–73.

Mango, Susan. "Alice in Two Wonderlands: Lewis Carroll in German." *Sub-stance* 16 (1977): 63–84.

Martinich, A. P. "A Theory of Communication and the Depth of Humor." *Journal of*

Literary Semantics 10, no. 1 (1981): 20–31.

Massey, Irving. *The Gaping Pig: Literature and Metamorphosis.* Berkeley: University of California Press, 1976.

Matthews, Charles. "Satire in the Alice Books." *Criticism* 12, no. 2 (1970): 105–19.

Morton, Lionel. "Memory in the Alice Books." *Nineteenth-Century Fiction* 33 (1978): 285–308.

Nagel, Ernest. "Symbolic Notation, Haddocks' Eyes, and the Dogwalking Ordinance." In *The World of Mathematics*, vol. 3, edited by J. R. Newman, 1878–1900. New York: Simon & Schuster, 1956.

Natov, Roni. "The Persistence of Alice." *The Lion and the Unicorn* 3, no. 1 (1979): 38–61.

Partridge, Eric. "The Nonsense Words of Edward Lear and Lewis Carroll." In *Here, There, and Everywhere*, 162–88. London: H. Hamilton, 1950.

Phillips, Robert, ed. *Aspects of Alice: Lewis Carroll's Dreamchild as Seen through the Critics' Looking-Glasses 1865–1971.* New York: Vanguard, 1971.

Polhemus, Robert M. *Comic Faith: The Great Tradition from Austen to Joyce.* Chicago: University of Chicago Press, 1980.

Pope, Randolph D., ed. *The Analysis of Literary Texts: Current Trends in Methodology.* 3rd and 4th York College Colloquia. Ypsilanti, Mich.: Bilingual Press, 1980.

Pudney, John. *Lewis Carroll and His World.* New York: Scribner's, 1976.

Quine, W. V. "Lewis Carroll's Logic." In *Theories and Things*, 134–42. Cambridge: Harvard University Press, 1981.

Rackin, Donald. "Corrective Laughter: Carroll's *Alice* and Popular Children's Literature of the Nineteenth Century." *Journal of Popular Culture* 1, no. 3 (1967): 243–55.

———, ed. Alice's Adventures in Wonderland: *A Critical Handbook.* Belmont, Calif.: Wadsworth Publishing, 1961.

Rapaport, Herman. "The Disarticulated Image: Gazing in Wonderland." *enclitic* 6, no. 2 (1982): 57–77.

Richardson, Joanna. *The Young Lewis Carroll.* London: Parrish, 1964.

Sale, Roger. *Fairy Tales and After: From Snow White to E. B. White.* Cambridge: Harvard University Press, 1978.

Sewell, Elizabeth. *The Field of Nonsense.* London: Chatto & Windus, 1952.

Shavit, Zohar. "The Ambivalent Status of Texts: The Case of Children's Literature." *Poetics Today* 1, no. 3 (1980): 75–86.

Shaw, John Mackay. *The Parodies of Lewis Carroll.* Talahassee: Florida State University Library, 1960.

Stewart, Susan. *Nonsense: Aspects of Intertextuality in Folklore and Literature.* Baltimore: Johns Hopkins University Press, 1979.

Stowell, Phyllis. "We're All Mad Here." *Children's Literature Association Quarterly* 8, no. 2 (1983): 5–8.

Suchan, James. "Alice's Journey from Alien to Artist." *Children's Literature* 7 (1978): 78–92.

Sutherland, Robert D. *Language and Lewis Carroll.* The Hague: Mounton, 1970.

Taylor, Alexander L. *The White Knight: A Study of C. L. Dodgson (Lewis Carroll).* Edinburgh: Oliver & Boyd, 1952.

Warren, Austin. "Carroll and His Alice Books." *The Sewanee Review* 88 (1980): 331–53.

Weaver, Warren. *Alice in Many Tongues: The Translations of* Alice in Wonderland.

Madison: University of Wisconsin Press, 1964.

———. "Lewis Carroll: Mathematician." *Scientific American* 194 (April 1956): 116–20.

———. "The Parrish Collection of Carrolliana." *Princeton University Library Chronicle* 17 (1956): 85–91.

Williams, Glanville L. "A Lawyer's *Alice*." *Cambridge Law Journal* 9, no. 2 (1946): 171–84.

Wood, James. *The Snark Was a Boojum: A Life of Lewis Carroll*. New York: Pantheon, 1966.

Acknowledgments

"Ironic Voyage" (originally entitled "Ironic Voyages") by Robert Martin Adams from *Nil: Episodes in the Literary Conquest of Void during the Nineteenth Century* by Robert Martin Adams, © 1966 by Robert Martin Adams. Reprinted by permission of Oxford University Press.

"The *Alice* Books and the Metaphors of Victorian Childhood" by Jan B. Gordon from *Aspects of Alice: Lewis Carroll's Dreamchild as Seen through the Critics' Looking-Glasses 1865-1971*, edited by Robert Phillips, © 1971 by the Vanguard Press, Inc. Reprinted by permission.

"Alice and Wonderland: A Curious Child" by Nina Auerbach from *Victorian Studies* 18, no. 1 (September 1973), ©1972 by the Trustees of Indiana University. Reprinted by permission.

"The Philosopher's *Alice*" (originally entitled "Introduction") by Peter Heath from *The Philosopher's Alice* with introduction and notes by Peter Heath, © 1974 by Peter Heath. Reprinted by permission of the author and St. Martin's Press.

"The *Sylvie and Bruno* Books as Victorian Novel" by Edmund Miller from *Lewis Carroll Observed: A Collection of Unpublished Photographs, Drawings, Poetry and New Essays*, edited by Edward Guiliano, © 1976 by Edward Guiliano. Reprinted by permission of the editor and Clarkson N. Potter, Inc.

"Carroll's *Alices*: The Semiotics of Paradox" by Alwin L. Baum from *American Imago* 34, no. 1 (Spring 1977), © by the Association for Applied Psychoanalysis, Inc. Reprinted by permission. The notes have been omitted.

"Plain Superficiality" by Judith Crews from *enclitic* 3, no. 2 (Fall 1979), © 1979 by *enclitic*. Reprinted by permission.

"Lewis Carroll, Laughter and Despair, and *The Hunting of the Snark*" (originally entitled "A Time for Humor: Lewis Carroll, Laughter and Despair, and *The Hunting of the Snark*") by Edward Guiliano from *Lewis Carroll: A Celebration: Essays on the Occasion of the 150th Anniversary of the Birth of Charles Lutwidge Dodgson*, © 1982 by Edward Guiliano. Reprinted by permission of the author and Clarkson N. Potter, Inc.

"Love and Death in Carroll's *Alices*" by Donald Rackin from *English Language Notes* 20, no. 2 (December 1982), © 1982 by the Regents of the University of Colorado. Reprinted by permission.

"Carroll's Well-Versed Narrative: *Through the Looking-Glass*" by Beverly Lyon Clark from *English Language Notes* 20, no. 2 (December 1982), © 1982 by the Regents of the University of Colorado. Reprinted by permission.

"Carroll's Quest Romance" by John Hollander, © 1987 by John Hollander. Published in this volume for the first time. Reprinted by permission of the author.

Index

Alice: and animals, 34–38, 44; as artist, 28, 29; deflation of love by, 112–13; as described by Carroll, 32, 113; as dreamer, 67; and fall down rabbit-hole, 72, 75–76, 77; as heroine, 50; identity of, 21–24, 26–27, 33–34, 35, 38, 72–73, 74, 77, 80, 81; maturity of, 3, 26; passivity of, 34–35; as *Pharmakos*, 74, 79; punishment of, 24; quest for queenhood of, 112–13; Tenniel's drawings of, 31–32; as Victorian child, 31. *See also* Liddell, Alice; *Alice's Adventures in Wonderland; Alice's Adventures under Ground; Through the Looking-Glass*

Alice's Adventures in Wonderland (Carroll): as adult literature, 51–52; as allegory, 3, 51, 69; animals in, 21, 34–36, 44, 114; as *Bildungsroman*, 30; Cheshire Cat in, 1, 2–4, 36–37, 70, 76, 79, 80, 84, 94–95, 112; as children's literature, 26–27; composition of, 47, 68, 123–24; concluding trial in, 44; crisis of, 5; and Darwinism, 18; death in, 118, 119, 120, 125–26; "doubleness" of, 23; and dreams, 66, 68, 70–71, 72, 77–78, 106, 142; etymology in, 97–98; and fairy tales, 24, 66, 67, 73; humor in, 110, 126, 129; *Hunting of the Snark* compared to, 103, 104; as logic-book, 51; love in, 111–21; Mad Hatter in, 4, 28–29, 36, 57, 74, 79, 94, 142; Mad Tea Party in, 4, 28, 36; memory in, 80–81; Mock Turtle in, 34, 35, 36, 38, 70, 76, 83, 94, 143, 145; names in, 84, 92–96;

narrative in, 138; nonsense in, 46–48, 51, 54–56, 69–70, 71, 113–14, 118–19, 126, 130; and nursery rhymes, 40, 112; paradox in, 66, 72, 76, 79, 81; parody in, 66, 72, 76, 79, 81; pessimism of, 108, 110; "Pig and Pepper" in, 1–4, 36, 145; popularity of, 65; pseudonyms in, 92–93; publication of, 18–19, 92; Queen of Hearts in, 78–79, 134, 144–45; as quest romance, 21, 23–24, 32, 49; role of verse in, 129, 130, 131, 133, 134, 135, 137, 138; semiotic structure of, 69, 74, 77, 78–79; space in, 72, 81; *Through the Looking-Glass* compared to, 5–6, 39, 142; time in, 5, 20, 57, 81, 106, 118, 125–26, 127; White Rabbit, 6, 75, 96, 106; Wonderland, 21, 23, 24, 28, 32, 37. *See also* Alice

Alice's Adventures under Ground, 36, 68, 112, 124, 127. *See also* Alice

"Alphabet Cipher, The" (Carroll), 100–102

Alter, Robert, 135

Andersen, Hans Christian, 141

Annotated Snark, The (Gardner), 14, 148, 150

Auden, W. H., 147, 148–49

Austen, Jane, 19, 43

Ayres, Harry Morgan, 142

Bab Ballads, The (Gilbert), 104

Badcock, Mary Hilton, 34

Barth, John, 66

Baudelaire, Charles, 14

Baum, L. Frank, 33

167

Beckett, Samuel, 66
Bentley, Richard, 148
Bergson, Henri, 109
Berman, Ruth, 57
Black, Duncan, 46
Blake, William, 112, 145
Bleak House (Dickens), 18, 22, 59
Boole, George, 46
Borges, Jorge Luis, 66, 81, 135, 148
Brontë, Charlotte, 44, 63
Brontë, Emily, 19, 59–60, 114
Browning, Robert, 4

Calvin, John, 42
Carlyle, Thomas, 126
Carroll, Lewis. *See* Dodgson, Charles Lutwidge
Carroll, Lewis (work of): as allegory, 3, 4, 51, 68, 69, 70; animals in, 21, 4, 34–35, 41, 44, 114; burlesque in, 130; and Darwinism, 17, 18, 36, 103, 112, 145; death in, 74, 105–6, 108, 110, 118, 119, 120, 125–26; and didactic verse, 131; displacement in, 79; and dreams, 55, 57, 66–68, 70–71, 72, 73, 75, 77–78, 106, 142, 146, 147; etymology in, 97–98, 146; and fairy tales, 24, 66, 67, 73; fictionality in, 135; game of Fort!/Da! in, 79; humor in, 103–4, 108, 109–10, 126, 129, 133, 136, 138–39; Edward Lear compared to, 48, 141; love in, 111–21; meaning in, 68, 69–70, 129–30; memory in, 80–81, 146; metaphor in, 71, 73, 80, 81; and modern fiction, 66, 138; names in, 83, 84, 91–96, 99–100; and nursery rhymes, 39–40, 112, 131, 134; overdetermination of, 66, 80; paradox in, 66, 71, 72, 76, 79, 81; paralogism in, 69, 72; parody in, 2, 4, 8, 81, 95–96, 129, 130–33, 138, 139, 142–43; as pastoral, 49; portmanteau words in, 69, 70, 77, 146, 147, 149; pronouns in, 95–96; proverbs in, 134; pseudonyms in, 92–93; quest in, 4, 15, 21, 23–24, 32, 49, 112–13, 115–16, 146, 147; regression in, 79; repression in, 21, 141–42; role of verse in, 129–39, 143; role of the voice in, 123; and

romanticism 4, 21, 23–24, 114–16, 142, 144, 146, 147, 151; sadomasochism in, 4, 27; sexual fantasy in, 66; space in, 20, 72, 73, 76–77, 81; time in, 5, 18–19, 20, 57, 73, 74, 76–77, 81, 106, 107, 118, 125–26, 127; unconscious in, 78; Victorian aspects of, 4, 17, 18, 31, 32, 103–104; women in, 42, 59, 148–49; word games in, 83–102. *See also* individual works
Cayley, Arthur, 45
Chambers, Robert, 17
Cohen, Mortin, 105
Coleridge, Samuel Taylor, 150
Collingwood, Stuart Dodgson, 38, 65, 70
Comus (Milton), 144
Contes (Perrault), 20
Coover, Robert, 138
Critique of Pure Reason (Kant), 49
Curiosa Mathematica (Carroll), 89–91, 109, 110

Darwin, Charles, 17–18, 19, 103, 112, 145
David Copperfield (Dickens), 19, 43, 59
de la Mare, Walter, 32, 37
De Morgan, Augustus, 46
Diana of the Crossways (Meredith), 18
Dickens, Charles, 18, 19, 22, 27, 32, 42, 43, 58, 59, 61, 62, 126
Disraeli, Benjamin, 145
Dobson, Austin, 34
Dr. Jekyll and Mr. Hyde (Stevenson), 23
Dodgson, Charles Lutwidge: Alice Liddell's relationship to, 33–34, 74; attitude toward animals of, 40; dislike of boys of, 32, 70; familiarity with comic writing of, 104; fear of death of, 105, 106–7, 108, 110; fondness for girls of, 32, 42, 66, 67, 111, 117, 119–21, 124–25; horror of eating of, 37–38, 70; insomnia of, 109; as "Lewis Carroll," 32, 46, 65, 92, 111; as logician, 46, 48, 50, 71–72; as mathematician, 45; social life of, 106; unconscious of, 110; as Victorian, 103–4; White Knight as self-portrait of, 8
Dombey and Son (Dickens), 43
Dostoevsky, Feodor, 24
"Doublets" (Carroll), 84–87